San Antonio Legacy

Folklore and Legends of a Diverse People

San Antonio Legacy

Folklore and Legends of a Diverse People

Donald E. Everett

Illustrated by José Cisneros

MAVERICK PUBLISHING COMPANY

MAVERICK PUBLISHING COMPANY
P.O. Box 6355, San Antonio, Texas 78209

First Trinity University Press edition 1979
First Maverick Publishing Company edition 1999

Library of Congress Cataloging-in-Publication Data

Everett, Donald E.
  San Antonio legacy : folklore and legends of a diverse people / Donald
E. Everett ; illustrated by José Cisneros.
    p. cm.
  Originally published: San Antonio : Trinity University Press, c1979.
  Includes index.
    ISBN 1-893271-11-0 (cloth : alk. paper) — ISBN 0-893271-12-9 (paper :
alk. paper)
    1. San Antonio (Tex.)—History—Anecdotes. 2. Legends—Texas—San
Antonio. I. Title.

F394.S2 E928 1999
976.4'351—dc21
                                                                    99-052386

08 07 06 05 04 03 02 01 00 99   10 9 8 7 6 5 4 3 2 1

Printed in the United States of America on acid-free paper

Contents

Preface

As have residents of other cities of significant historical interest, San Antonians have inherited a collection of legends and folk tales. These pages recall the exploits of the good men and the bad men one expects to find in the record of any frontier town.

But there are unexpected paradoxes which may help us understand why San Antonio has been for so long such a singular attraction.

Nationally regarded as a center of industrial indolence and perhaps the last town of consequence to boast of a railway line, San Antonio had, a decade before the railroad, a commercial ice factory second only to one in New Orleans. Known as a haven for ungodly men, its citizens of all faiths have always had a special attachment to its missions. Famous throughout the Southwest for the products of German-born brewers, one of that national background "invented" the first ice cream soda. Regarded as somnolent with little interest in progress, it was the setting for the first successful demonstration of barbed wire, an event that changed the life of the entire Southwest.

Among the popular images of Texas and the Southwest, however, one is missing. In the pages of the *San Antonio Express* from 1865 to 1929, the reader rarely comes across a "tall tale." If one is reported, as in the champagne bath at the Menger Hotel, it is likely to have been written by an outsider determined to describe some aspect of the San Antonio scene in terms of the author's preconceived ideas. That may be just as well.

No outsider, and few natives, will ever fully understand a town where such a conglomerate collection of stories could emanate from such a polyglot population. San Antonio's is an unlikely legacy.

Inconsistencies in spelling and typography appear throughout these stories. Glaring errors have been corrected and punctuation has been added or deleted for clarity. Even so, archaic, and/or defective sentence structure is sometimes distracting today. Accent marks and tildes were not to be found in the printers' fonts at the *Express* and have been added herein. Scholars are forewarned to check the original sources for direct quotations.

Lois Boyd, Joe Nicholson and Virginia Cabello of the old Trinity University Press contributed their special expertise to the original edition of this collection of San Antoniana, which was supported by Patsy and Marshall Steves and in this new edition is still enhanced by the artistic talent of José Cisneros.

Part I
Frontier Town

Under the flags of five nations San Antonio retained its role as "marketplace of the borderlands," an unheralded sobriquet that has more realistic and enduring meaning than slogans conjured up by latter-day publicists. Whether for Mexican carretas or for the stagecoaches and wagon trains of the Anglo-American, its plazas have served as both departure and destination points for countless frontier travelers.

The frontiersman's leisure time often revolved around gambling and intoxicants. Nearly 300 bars and saloons by 1892 provided important sources of income for local citizens. While the "Champagne Bath" is an aprocryphal story, the "Gaming Tables" account represents a fair measure of truth. Of fortunes won and lost at gaming tables, writer Frank Bushick noted that local apologists for gambling insisted that "it kept money in circulation."

Local tradition, buttressed in recent years by a state historical marker, has acknowledged Military Plaza as the site of the first successful demonstration of barbed wire. W. D. Hornaday's interview in 1910 with John W. Gates's associate Pete McManus clearly indicates that this historical event took place on Alamo Plaza in 1876. In retrospect, one can readily see that the steady procession of man and beast on Military Plaza would have precluded a demonstration of range cattle in a corral at that location. Removed from the mainstream of business activity, only Alamo Plaza, a "mudhole" as McManus remembered it, offered ample space.

Another product, ice, was a luxury in early San Antonio. Prior to the Civil War only the very affluent could afford this precious item, brought south by steamship to Indianola and then by oxcart to the city. Indeed, the masses could not afford the price of the first commercially manufactured ice. It was the prohibitive price of ice that led G. A. Duerler to "invent" the ice cream soda.

Local progress could be exemplified in the public as well as the private sector, and nowhere so readily as in the evolution of the fire department. While the volunteer fire associations were assuredly private organizations, they served a public need. As elsewhere in the nation, one's social status might well correlate to the fire company to which one belonged. It was not until the last decade of the century that the city assumed responsibility for this service to its citizens.

The rule of the vigilantes in frontier San Antonio, while of brief duration, was but one of the excesses of the post–Civil War period. San Antonians are generally familiar with the story of the ten men hung in one day by the vigilantes despite the protestations of Bishop Dubuis, who later cut down ten beautiful China trees in front of his Military Plaza residence to prevent the recurrence of this horrendous scene. The details of the lynching of Bob Augustine, a well-known badman, are less familiar. This vivid childhood memory was recalled by Charles A. Herff, son of the renowned Dr. Ferdinand Herff.

San Antonio's Catholic heritage is represented here by two diverse areas of the city, only one of which would be recognizable to the uninformed. The Chapel of the Miracles yet stands at the same location, seemingly as isolated as ever. Built to shelter a statue brought from Spain in the eighteenth century, the chapel remains a shrine for those who pray for miracles. By way of contrast, thousands of people daily cross the Campo Santo, not knowing that they are treading on holy ground. Recent discussions about the exact location of Ben Milam's tomb have prompted some misleading statements about the Campo Santo. The accompanying article should clarify the misunderstandings.

1.
Stagecoach Travel

From the early newspapers printed in San Antonio and from accounts of experiences written by stagecoach drivers, one can learn a great many interesting details of travel in Texas in the 1850s.

In the *San Antonio Ledger* for May 22, 1851, an advertisement announced the beginning of a new triweekly stageline between San Antonio and Austin. There was no display advertising at that time; advertisements were set up in the same way as news. A small cut of a stagecoach appeared on the first line at the extreme left.

> The Proprietor respectfully informs the traveling public that he has fully organized this Line and is now prepared to carry passengers between Austin and San Antonio. He has provided pleasant and convenient coaches, good and fresh teams, and skillful and accommodating drivers. He will make the trip through in one day.
>
> No visitor to the State should fail to pass over this route as it leads through one of the most beautiful portions of Texas, by way of San Marcos and New Braunfels. This line connects at Austin with the Line to Houston and that to Gonzales, and at New Braunfels with the Line to La Vaca Bay.
>
> Leaving Austin every Tuesday, Thursday and Saturday morning, will reach San Antonio the same evening, and returning leave San Antonio every Monday, Wednesday and Friday morning and arrive at Austin the same evenings. Fare through $6. From Austin to San Marcos, $2.50; from San Marcos to New Braunfels, $1.50; from New Braunfels to San Antonio, $2.00. Captain A. Coleman is agent at San Antonio; Colonel Durham at San Marcos, and Captain J. M. W. Hall at Austin. No seat will be considered engaged until the name is registered and the fare paid. J. S. Harrison, Proprietor.

In this ad "He will make the trip through in one day" was in boldface type. Evidently it was something new to make the 80-mile trip in one day. One cannot help compare the coaches with today's buses, which make the trip from Austin to San Antonio in three hours and charge less than one-half as much as the stage drivers did. In the *San Antonio Texan* on February 21, 1856, was this ad:

Between San Antonio and Eagle Pass, via Castroville, Quihi, D'Hanis, and Leona, leaving San Antonio every Monday at 6 o'clock, a.m., and arrives at San Antonio on Saturday at 4 o'clock, p.m. Office at Edward Braden's. A. David, Proprietor.

Another ad read:

From San Antonio to Seguin, $3.00; San Antonio to Gonzales, $6.50; from San Antonio to Victoria, $10.00; from San Antonio to Indianola, $12.50; from Indianola to Victoria, $3.00; from Indianola to Gonzales, $6.50; from Indianola to Seguin, $10.00, and from Indianola to San Antonio, $12.50.

For further information apply to C. R. Jamison, San Antonio; J. L. Nickelson, Victoria agent; J. L. Allen, proprietor, Indianola.

Indianola was an important port, and the stagecoach from San Antonio met a ship line there. . . . Notice of the boat line's inauguration was in the *San Antonio Ledger* on Thursday, May 22, 1851. Many supplies . . . were brought from the northern states in ships to Indianola and transported overland in a stagecoach or a wagon to San Antonio, the distributing center.

The people of Western Texas are informed that a permanent and regular line of ships has been established between the City of Philadelphia and Indianola, Texas, to run monthly at least, and semi-monthly or weekly as the trade may require. From six to 10 vessels will be on the line. They are large, spacious and commanded by experienced seamen. By this line the merchants of Texas have offered to them the best of market in the Union, for all agricultural implements, boots, shoes, iron, casting, hats, caps, woolen and assorted merchandise. A fine field is offered for emigration from Pennsylvania and the neighboring states.

An idea of the merchandise imported to Texas by way of this port can be gained from an advertisement of June 12, 1851:

Just received by the line of packets lately established to run between Philadelphia and Matagorda Bay a Large Assortment of Goods, Wares, merchandise, and Implements for Agricultural Purposes, which will be sold

to Merchants and planters by wholesale, and at reduced prices. The assortment consists of Dry Goods of all descriptions. Hardware, cutlery, queensivory by the crate, combs and brushes, looking-glasses, fine soaps, hats, caps, boots, shoes, drugs, etc. Best Pennsylvania ploughs, sub-soil ploughs, harrows, cultivators, corn-shellers, scythes, and sneads, hay-forks, spades, axes, etc.

Persons wishing to purchase can be suited, as ready means for having shipped to this Bay all kinds of goods is at hand and all articles wanted will be sent to order immediately from Philadelphia.

Many people from San Antonio must have gone to Indianola to buy and sell goods, meet ships and get a boat to Philadelphia, for a number of Indianola firms carried regular advertisements in San Antonio papers. One particularly interesting one for a hotel in Indianola can be found in the *Western Texan* on September 30, 1852:

The undersigned, having leased the above property heretofore so favorably known, and having given it a thorough renovating throughout, besides repapering, painting and furnishing with entire new furniture, is now ready to accommodate those who may favor him with a call. He also pledges himself to spare no pains or expense whatever to make those calling on him as comfortable as at any hotel in Western Texas. Families or other persons visiting Indianola will find the rooms at the Planter's Hotel comfortable, and the table supplied with as good eating as the market and country will afford. But as it is much easier to make promises than to redeem them, please call and examine for yourselves. William M. Varnell.

The longest stageline in this part of the country then was from San Antonio to Santa Fe, New Mexico. It took an entire month, and the fare for the whole journey was $125. It cost $100 from El Paso to San Antonio and $30 from Santa Fe to El Paso. Each passenger was allowed 40 pounds of baggage. The coach left Santa Fe on the second of every other month and arrived at San Elizario on the 11th. Leaving San Elizario on the 12th, it arrived in San Antonio on the last day of the same month. The distance between watering places was nowhere greater than 40 miles. Mr. Henry Skillman, the driver, was advertised as an old hand at . . . running stagecoaches and as thoroughly familiar with the route.

— *San Antonio Express*, October 29, 1929

2.
Silver and Cotton Shipments

Frederick Groos, the founder of F. Groos & Co., came to Texas in 1848, and in 1854 founded the business that until Friday morning existed under the one name. He was a clerk in the banking and mercantile house of Bryan Callaghan, Sr., the father of the present mayor of San Antonio, when the elder Callaghan was in business in Eagle Pass. Frederick left Callaghan's employ and started in business for himself at Eagle Pass, taking into partnership Carl and Gustav Groos. A merchandise and banking business was started with a capital of $2,000, and the firm of F. Groos & Co. did a continuous business until the first of this month, when, the charter being received from the Comptroller of the Currency, the name was changed to the Groos National Bank. . . .

The business in its early days in Eagle Pass was largely mercantile like most of the old-time private banking firms, but year by year the bank end was slowly developing so that in 1874 the firm was transferred to San Antonio.

In those days the principal duties were not only in receiving and caring for deposits but in having to do with conversion of gold and silver and dealing in Mexican silver, most of the commerce being in Mexican silver dollars. In the banking rooms now are relics of these "primitive" days, and until a few years ago an old safe that had seen long and hard service stood in the vault. This safe was built in a special fashion to accommodate the heavy wooden boxes sealed, in which the silver would be shipped.

This has gone the way of all old and wornout furniture, but objects of curiosity to the younger generation and of familiar aspect recalling old faces and customs to many of the old clients of the

Groos bank are still retained in the shape of the ancient gold scales, the boxes, one inch thick, where the money was shipped, the boxes of weights like a jeweler uses ranging from a pennyweight up and the old money scale on which silver in bulk was weighed, 1,000 silver dollars weighing 59 3/4 pounds.

In the Eagle Pass and the early San Antonio banking days money was transported hidden carefully in the center of cotton bales, or in secret receptacles in the axles of the Mexican "caritas," or carts. These enormous axles were made of wood. Holes would be bored in and packed with silver dollars, a wooden plug at the opening effectively concealing the riches within. This was such a splendid hiding place that the numerous bandits and badmen were outwitted and the secret was kept to the joy of the bankers.

The old leather-covered ledgers show many financial transactions between one of the richest men of Mexico, Everisto Madero, the late grandfather of the present president of Mexico, and F. Groos & Co. Before the day of the iron safe, money was kept in large dry goods boxes wrapped around with iron hoops which were riveted to the wood. This was also an effective way, as the boxes were too large for robbers to carry off unless in force and they could not be broken up and rifled without creating such a racket the watchman would hear them. All the books having to do with the accounts were made with three different value columns, one for gold, another for silver and a third for currency. . . .

An interesting story is told by Franz Groos of the first considerable shipment of cotton ever made from San Antonio out of the boundary line of the United States. This was in 1862 when Julius Maureau undertook to transport to Mexico 750 bales of cotton for Mr. Groos's grandfather, F. Maureau of New Braunfels, whose portion was 250 bales, and for H. Meyer 250 bales and F. Groos & Co. 250 bales, or 750 bales in all. The shipment was taken in caritas from San Antonio to Saltillo, Mexico, where even in those days were spinning mills. Mr. Maureau hoped that he would be able to sell at a good profit, but found the price offered, 25 cents a pound, entirely too small.

He continued on with the cotton, arriving in San Luis Potosi, which, he believed, would be a better market. In this town he ran ac-

J. CISNEROS

ross one of the Chabots of the well-known San Antonio family, who advised him to continue with his cotton to the City of Mexico, since in San Luis Potosi, while he could dispose of it, the buyer would take it on to the city and make a profit that could just as well jingle in the pockets of Mr. Maureau.

The San Antonian arrived in the City of Mexico with his heavy caravan after many minor adventures on the way. Here in the capital he sold the load at 56 cents a pound [in] Mexican silver dollars, which then were even more valuable than the silver dollar of the United States. As Mexico was in the throes of a revolution and the silver was such a load, and transportation for it in safety a stupendous problem, he finally bought exchange from the City of Mexico to San Luis Potosi at 8 per cent premium.

From San Luis Potosi that money was transported in corn sacks, guarded by a small cavalcade that finally arrived in San Antonio safely, after having been gone about six months. The profit on the transaction was $56,000 which was divided as follows: Julius Maureau took half, since he had transported the cotton and sold it, while the other half was divided between the consignors.

— *San Antonio Express*, March 3, 1912

3.
Wagon Trains

Among the old frontiersmen now living in San Antonio is Capt. William Edgar, United States ex-vice-consul to Mexico. He was called upon by a reporter for the *Express* and requested to recount some of his experiences on the Texas frontier and in Mexico and give reminiscences of wagon train life in the great Southwest.

Capt. Edgar came to Texas in August 1845 as a United States soldier under Gen. Zachary Taylor. Texas was not annexed to the United States until the 7th day of December following, a fact not generally known. On the 8th of March 1846, the army moved to the Rio Grande and thence through the war with Mexico. The captain said:

In 1848 at the close of the Mexican war, six companies of my old regiment, the Third United States Infantry, were ordered to Texas. The winter of 1848 and 1849 was spent in camp on the Salado near San Antonio. In the spring of 1849 the six companies with a large supply train left San Antonio for El Paso accompanied by a large number of civilians, many of them in the employ of then Col. Joseph E. Johnston of Confederate fame. Col. Johnston was the United States topographical engineer and charged with opening a military road from San Antonio to El Paso.

We were ninety days in reaching our destination. The road was immediately put in use for commercial purposes and continued as such up to 1879, when the advent of railroads broke up wagon traffic. From 1850 to 1879 all freights for El Paso, Chihuahua and all northwest Texas and northeastern Mexico went over the route in well-organized trains, but the men were poorly armed with ancient muzzle-loading guns with very few repeating arms of any description, and then only found in the hands of wagon masters.

The road ran through Castroville, D'Hanis, Quihi and Fort Inge at first; later on it was changed further south and went from Castroville to D'Hanis, thence to Uvalde. From this latter place there was no house or habitation for over 550 miles, the first being San Elizario, on the Rio Grande thirty miles south of El Paso. The government later on established the posts of Fort Clark, Camp Hudson, Camp Lancaster, Fort Stockton, Fort Davis and Fort Quitman, which gave better protection to trains.

Prior to the establishment of these posts the Indians were numerous and very troublesome, but usually found in small bodies and unable to cope with trainmen, but frequently following in the wake of trains picking up a stray bear hunter or stealing mules when a favorable opportunity would offer. They would often approach trains in early times under cover of a flag of truce and under pretext of begging for something to eat, would usually endeavor to possess information over your movements, as to when the men slept, how they guarded, how many there were, how armed and where going. After their departure the greatest vigilance became necessary to avoid a surprise, as you were almost certain to be visited if you relaxed in the least your vigilance.

I followed the road as wagonmaster first for Lewis & Groesbeck, and later on for L. and G. P. Devine, from 1851 to 1855. When with Lewis and Groesbeck, my train consisted of only six wagons and nine men all told, badly armed. Once or twice I was surrounded by Indians but not attacked, while they kept up their war songs throughout the entire night in close proximity. . . .

Before the Civil War broke out between the States there were only four trains on the road. Among them were those known as I. D. Burges, Bill Smith, Joe Devine's, Deguere's, William McHenry's and McCoomb's. Six regular freighters, now and then a train from Mexico or New Mexico, would drop in and make a trip, then leave for other parts.

In 1865, or at the close of the Civil War, a great many trains were put on the road, among which were Froboese and Shihagen, Banns and Edgar, Roy Bean, Santiago, Talmantez, Santleben,

Gonzales, Ochod, Crossen, Walker, Vincent, Holly, beside which Adams and Wickes became government contractors, and under said contract they were required to organize and handle their own trains. They put on 14 trains of 10 wagons each, as follows: 10 trains of 10-mule wagons, 2 trains of 14-mule wagons, 2 trains of 8-mule wagons. Besides this they had 2 cart trains of 25 carts each with 3 yokes of oxen to the cart.

Ox teams were not a success on this road owing to the great distance between water, to wit: from the first crossing of Devil's river to the second crossing, 40 miles, no certain water; from Beaver Lake to Howard Springs, 43 miles; from Howard to Live Oak Creek, 37 miles; from Comanche Springs to Limpia Creek, 45 miles; from head of Limpia Creek to Barrel Springs, 21 miles; Barrel Springs to Eagle Springs, 67 miles; Eagle Springs to Rio Grande, 39 miles. At times water would be found at intermediate points, but often insufficient and unreliable.

The usual time from San Antonio to El Paso was 40 to 50 days, and 30 days returning, round trip 80 days.

— *San Antonio Express*, September 23, 1894

4.
A Champagne Bath

A correspondent of the *St. Louis Globe-Democrat* was in San Antonio during the Cattlemen's convention to get material for a real Texas cowboy story. He found out there was rough country between Alpine and the Rio Grande and, inquiring around for the names of a few cattlemen who were in business down on the lower Rio Grande years ago, someone gave him the name of Captain King and Sam Wolcott.

So he has a man 76 years old from out in Brewster county who has just been roping some wild steers on his ranch [the fictional Jim Gregory] serve as narrator. Thus the following about "real cowboys":

It's a heap different ridin' to San Antonio from way out here on a railroad passenger train than it was a-making the trip in the days before the railroad was built, said Jim Gregory, who has been ranching down below the Turney pasture for the last 30 years and more.

In them days we felt like a good time was a-comin' to us when we got to the end of our trip. Every cow represented a big bunch of money, and we were not troubled about grazin' on some other feller's land or made to pay back lease money to the state like we are now. The railroads killed the cattle business, there ain't no two ways about it. It brought the farmers and land men and they brought the wire fences, and the wire fences stopped free grazin'. In them early times every day was like a cowman's convention in San Antonio. They were gathered there from all over the Southwest, an' they was rollin' in money, I'm here to tell you. I was nothin'

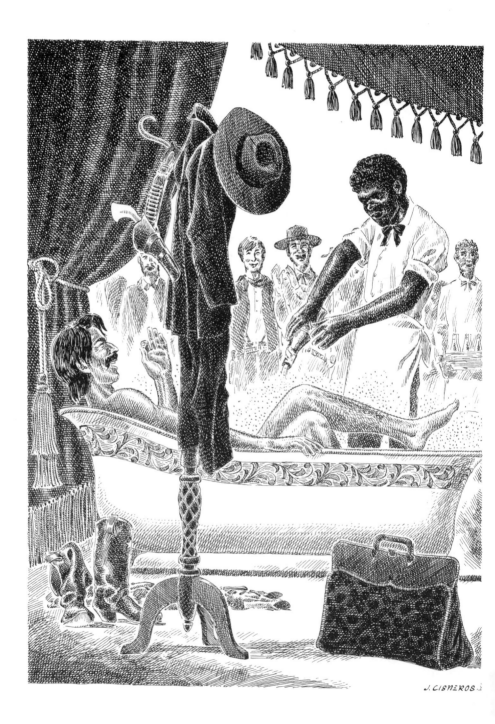

but a cowpuncher then myself, but I saw some high rollin' times along with the 'cow barons,' as the newspapers used to call 'em. Champagne flowed like water when such men as King and Maverick and a hundred others of the same kind got into town.

I remember I was loafin' around the Menger hotel one hot day in summer. I'd been in town for three or four days and was about through with my spree when the stage from Laredo rolled up and out falls old man Wolcott—we called everybody old man—he wasn't more'n 30, I guess. He hadn't been in from his Rio Grande ranch for six months or more. It had been a hot and dusty ride for 150 miles, and he felt the need of bein' invigorated. . . .

'Come on, boys,' he sang out as he greeted the dozen or more cowmen lounging in the shade of the hackberry trees in front of the hotel. We all knew that meant an invitation to take a drink. 'Give me the best room you got in the house,' he yelled to the clerk as we filed past the desk into the barroom. 'An' don't forget I want one with a big bathtub.'

'I've been down in the God-forsaken country making money and ain't had a bath for six months,' he told us as we lined up waiting to have our poison set before us. 'I've been a-thinkin' about it on my ride up here, and have decided to take a bath that is a bath.'

'I've heard that San Antonio water does first rate for bathing purposes,' said someone in the crowd. 'Water hell!' Wolcott exclaimed. 'I'm a-goin' to bathe in champagne.'

He meant just what he said. When we had finished takin' our drinks he ordered enough champagne to fill up one of them big old-fashioned bathtubs up to within two or three inches of the top. I don't know how many bottles it took. . . . When the tub was full, Wolcott stripped off and got in. He sent out and bought a whole outfit of new clothes. He wallowed around in that champagne for an hour or two and then dressed up in his new clothes. He told us fellers it was the finest bath he ever had an' we agreed that it ought to be good, for it had cost enough.

The crowd of old-time stockmen sat silent for a moment. They were calling up memories of the past.

'Times have changed most wonderful in the last 15 or 20 years,' said one of the group. 'In the old days if a man had the money and wanted to take a flyer at roulette or any other kind of game, he had plenty of chances to do it in San Antonio, an' nobody thought or cared anything about it. I've seen cowmen lose ten to twenty thousand dollars in one night down at the Silver King or the Crystal, an' never bat an eyelash. I've seen the same men win that much in one night and spend it all before they got out of town.

'Nickel picture shows is the most excitin' thing they've got there now, so I'm told. I've got a whole dollar to spend in dissipation, an' I'm a-goin' to take in every durned 5-cent show in town.'

— San Antonio Express, May 18, 1908

5.
Barbed Wire Man

Pete P. McManus, who has the record of having sold many times more barbed wire than any man in the world, retired from business a few days ago. He was sent to Texas 33 years ago with John W. Gates to give practical demonstrations of the new fencing material.

Mr. Gates quickly saw the possibility of big profits from the manufacture of the wire, and, taking advantage of the opportunity, made an enormous fortune out of the industry in a few years. Mr. McManus was contented to remain with the sales department in these years, making his headquarters at San Antonio most of the period. Mr. McManus said:

Barbed wire fences have done more to civilize and develop the Southwest and West than any other influences. . . . In Texas alone the building of these fences has caused millions and millions of dollars of wealth to be added to the state by making it possible for the unoccupied lands to be settled and converted into farms. But for the invention and use of barbed wire for fences, the vast scope of grazing lands in Texas and the West would still be an open range. To farm these lands under such conditions would be out of the question. Fences could not have been built out of rails, as that would have been too expensive.

It is safe to assert that the use of barbed wire for fences has placed Texas and the West 25 to 30 years ahead of what they otherwise would have been in progress and development. Of course, it is barely possible that some other kind of cheap fencing material might have been invented, but I cannot conceive what it could be.

This fencing up of the ranchlands was followed by dividing the ranches into farming tracts. Then came the building of railroads, the establishment of towns and various kinds of industries. But for the building of barbed wire fences, the setting up of an enormous territory of this country would have been impossible.

In the days when all of Western and Southwestern Texas was an open range, it was comparatively easy for bands of cattle thieves and other outlaws to carry on their operations with little danger of capture. The fencing up of the open range with barbed wire had more to do with bringing the reign of the cattle thieves to a close than the State Rangers, and, in saying this, I do not mean to detract in the slightest degree the good work performed by the Rangers. But it was simply impossible for the thieves to run off the cattle in the way they did before the range was fenced. In the days of free and open range, the outlaws could round up and drive a herd of cattle off across country, following some isolated trail, but they found it hard work to get away after the fences were built.

I believe that much of the barbed wire fence cutting which caused so much excitement in the western part of Texas in the '80s was done chiefly by cattle thieves and not by the 'free-grass' ranchmen. Of course, the fencing of the open range was opposed by some of the cattlemen; they were not opposed to the innovation as much as the outlaws who had been used to carrying on their operations unhampered.

What are the circumstances connected with the introduction of barbed wire for fencing purposes? Mr. McManus was asked. [He replied:]

To begin with, barbed wire is not an American invention. It was first invented and manufactured in Germany. A man named Glidden got the idea in Germany and began the manufacture of the wire on a small scale in this country.

It was in 1876 that John W. Gates and I came to Texas for the purpose of demonstrating the practicality of the wire for fencing purposes. We went to San Antonio, taking several reels of wire with us. We made our first demonstration upon Alamo Plaza for the benefit of a crowd of cattlemen who were gathered there from different parts of Southwest Texas. At that time, Alamo Plaza was a mudhole. Mr. Gates and I set up the posts and strung four strands of barbed wire, making a corral of considerable size. Some of the cowboys were skeptical, and Gates and I were jollied a good deal as we went about our work of preparing for the test. A bunch of range cattle were driven into the corral and the ranchmen expected to see them go through or over the fence, but the wires held them without any trouble.

Mr. Gates and I gave other demonstrations of the practicality of the fencing material and took some good orders for the wire. That was really the beginning of the barbed wire industry. Mr. Gates saw that it was a good thing and he began its manufacture.

— W. D. Hornaday, *San Antonio Express*, February 27, 1910

6.

Ice Cream Sodas

Few people know that [the] ice cream soda was invented in San Antonio. Fewer people, perhaps, know that its inventor is a distinguished citizen of this city, and that the necessity that was the mother of this invention was occasioned by the high price of ice in San Antonio some twenty-five years ago.

Here are the facts.

G. A. Duerler Sr., the man who popularized shelled pecans and who taught Texas to eat candy, operated in connection with his candy manufacturing business a soda water fountain. It was a summer in the early '80s. The weather was extremely hot and the price of ice was very high. Indeed, it was so high that it was a problem to Mr. Duerler to keep his soda water cold and at the same time make a profit on it. He schemed and schemed but could find no way out of the difficulty.

Then one day the idea came to him suddenly: why not try to cool each glass of soda water with a little ice cream? That would be a little cheaper than ice.

How would ice cream taste in soda water, anyway? To think with Mr. Duerler was to act, as they say in the story books, and soon he made the first glass of ice cream soda! Lovers of ice cream soda can imagine his delight when he tasted it. He realized immediately that he had accidentally hit upon a new drink, and decided to try it on the first of his friends who came into the place.

It happened that the first one to come in was Henry Radaz, at that time the postmaster of the city. Mr. Radaz was forthwith induced to try this new concoction, and his verdict was that it was "perfectly delicious."

"Why, that is a fine new drink," said Mr. Radaz. "You ought to give it a name."

"Well, what name do you think would suit?" asked Mr. Duerler.

It was the time when the Dolly Varden dresses were the rage, and quick as a flash Mr. Radaz answered: "Why, call it 'Dolly Varden!'"

And "Dolly Varden" it was. It took like wildfire. Soon everybody in San Antonio was drinking [a] "Dolly Varden." The drummers who traveled into the city in those days took the news of the new drink with a description of how it was made to other sections of the country and it was not long until "Dolly Varden" was being sold in every large city in the United States. It is only in recent years, with the coming of a new generation, that the people of San Antonio have become accustomed to speaking of "ice cream soda" instead of using the original name. Old San Antonio will recall the name, but it will be news to them that the drink that bore it was invented by Mr. Duerler.

— *San Antonio Express*, April 6, 1913

7.

The Firemen

Yellow, the writing a little faded by the half century and more that has passed since the words were penned; frayed at the folds, the edges sadly tattered, the oldest existing record of the fire department very fitly reposes in the care of the oldest fireman. . . .

On December 24, 1850—this from the records—a meeting was called for the purpose of organizing an "East Side Hose Company," . . . M. G. Cotton being in the chair.

They came right to the point in those primitive days and the minutes of the first meeting show a refreshing, delightful dearth of parliamentary drivel. A Mr. Riall was chosen vice president and Daniel L. McGary secretary. The announcement that $2,000 was already pledged the new organization was then made.

"The Alamo Fire Association No. 2" was the name chosen for the new organization and W. A. Menger, C. Byrne, R. D. Stumberg and D. L. McGary were appointed a committee on constitution and by-laws, to report at the next meeting.

Luckily, though there was $2,000, there was no budget to contend with; so, not being perplexed by matters financial, the members met the following evening in the Menger Hotel, prepared for business.

On a motion by Mr. Marshall, Peter Gallagher was elected chief, W. A. Menger assistant chief, D. L. McGary secretary, Stephen Danenhauer treasurer, and officers authorized to secure a charter . . . and operate their little engine.

Two long ropes stretched from the front of the engine, with hand-grips attached at intervals. As the department was an "all San Antonio" affair and everybody [a] helper, whether a regular member or no, every trade and profession might be seen represented as the members cavorted madly down the street, the engine clattering in their wake.

Innocent bystanders recall the fact that it was particularly edifying to see the companies responding to a night alarm in various stages of dishabille. Even more so on a night when a dance or reception was being held, and when guarache pattered side by side with patent leather pump, wide-brimmed sombrero jostled scant-brimmed top hat, gaily colored "vanda" contrasting with gleaming shirt front, with here and there a nightshirt streaming in the wind, telling of some citizen less gay and festive disturbed from his restful couch.

It lay within the province of the foreman of an engine company to commandeer the nearest team of horses and attach them to the engine, the owner being tendered $5 for the service. . . .

San Antonio was a precocious town and in 1867 began putting on metropolitan airs. So the department decided that it would have a steamer instead of the old "back-breakers." And have a steamer it did. The engine came by water to Indianola and thence to San Antonio by wagon train, and reached the city in September, 1868. It was tested on Main Plaza—the population of San Antonio acting as volunteer inspection committee—in front of San Fernando church, water being pumped from the acequia that ran beneath the steps. . . .

When an alarm sounded—of which alarm more anon—the engines were run to the ditch, river, creek, or well, the suction pipe dropped and the hose—it was of leather in fifty-feet sections, in those days—stretched to the threatened building. In the event the house was too far from water for the hose to reach, the water was "relayed."

One engine would lay its hose as far as it would reach in the direction of the fire. There was placed a hogshead or a large barrel, into which the hose discharged. The suction hose of the second engine was thrust in and the water sent further on its journey.

In the days of the hand-pump engines the game was this: One company got red in the face trying to make the barrel overflow; the other striving mightily to run it dry—all to the sound of strange lurid words in Teutonic and Gaelic dialects, punctuated with many a sibilant "Sapriati!," explosive "Caramba!" or suavely profane "Mon Dieu!". . . .

Sunday mornings were set aside for trials, and the hook and ladder men quickly gained a great degree of efficiency. Every man being an athlete, the truck always made good time and their work with the ladders enhanced the work of the pipemen.

Despite the dearth of great buildings in the '60s and '70s there raged many a large fire that was successfully combated by the volunteers. But there was none so spectacular as the one known as the "Alamo fire," which occurred in the early part of 1874.

It was a Sunday afternoon and a quiet, drowsy day. Dinner had long since been eaten and the greater portion of the population were indulging in a quiet siesta. Suddenly the somnolent silence was shattered by a raucous "dang-dang-dang" from the bell of No. 2, signifying that a fire was in progress in the Third Ward. There is a slight discrepancy in the statements of old members—the records are strangely silent on this point—some claiming that the bell rang, not "dang-dang-dang" but "dong-dong-dong." As the bell of No. 2 was a large one, however, it is safe to say that the tune was deep and the latter are correct in saying the signal was "dong-dong-dong". . .

Volumes of smoke rising from the northeast corner of Alamo Plaza discovered to the department [that] the long, two-story building occupied then by Honoré Grenet's store and warehouse [was] a mass of flames. The feed pipes of the engines were quickly attached to the Alamo Madre Ditch and soon water was being thrown on the flames.

Gus Mauermann and Ferdinand Herff, members of the Turner Hook and Ladder Truck Company, carried a line of hose to a portion of the shingle roof not yet ablaze. Mauermann, on taking his station on the roof, had removed his shoes to obtain a foothold on the slippery incline. In endeavoring to reach them, preparatory to dragging the hose to another portion of the roof, he missed his footing on the moss-covered shingles, rendered still more treacherous by the water, and slipped sprawling to the eaves. Here he managed to catch a projection and hung dangling from the gutter.

A shout went up from the crowd that had by this time filled the plaza, and Bernhardt Mauermann, Gail Borden, George Caen and a

J. CISNEROS

lightning-red agent by the name of Spencer sprang to aid the pendant volunteer. He retained his hold for a moment, then dropped to the ground thirty feet below. His fall was broken by the men below, and he sustained but a fractured instep—from the effects of which, however, he suffers at times today.

In the meantime, a breeze had carried flaming bits of shingles across the plaza, there to fall on the roof of the old Maverick homestead, on the site of the Gibbs Building. A detachment of firemen at once hurried to the new danger point, where another volunteer was injured and Henry Schaefer of the Turner Hook and Ladder narrowly escaped a fatal or serious accident. . . . The Maverick homestead was but slightly charred, while the Grenet premises, despite the headway the fire had gained before it was discovered, was saved. . . .

In the old days there were bells at No. 1 and No. 2 engine houses. The first person to discover a fire ran to the nearest bell, there to sound the alarm. . . . The bell would be rung, the number of the ward in which the fire was situated being announced by the taps, one for Ward 1, and so on. Arriving within the confines of the ward, the company inquired politely but firmly the exact location. The etiquette of the occasion required the following formula by the foreman of the company: "Ou ist the lumore? Lead me to it!" or words to that effect. The small boy was as much in evidence in those days as now, so difficulty was never experienced.

— Solon K. Stewart, *San Antonio Express*, September 10, 1911

8.

The Lynching of Bob Augustine

To understand the following story, I will have to give you a succinct description of conditions in San Antonio some 65 years ago. It was then only a small frontier town, with about 8,000 inhabitants, but considered a well-behaved and law-abiding town until about the outbreak of and during the Civil War, when many undesirables drifted in. Horse thieves, gamblers, cutthroats and desperadoes bore full sway. Intimidation was resorted to; lawyers, judges, officers of the law, and prospective jurors shirked their duties.

At last things became intolerable and a vigilance committee was organized to wipe out these conditions. Three hundred of the best citizens joined this organization to take the law into their own hands. They acted energetically and swiftly, and in about two weeks 20 or more badmen were lynched. This had a salubrious effect and San Antonio became a habitable place.

The story concerns the lynching of Bob Augustine, which I unfortunately witnessed as a small boy. It was a terrible event in my life. It made an indelible impression on my mind, and I shall never be able to forget. I think it will not be amiss if I give you a description of the main actors in the drama.

Bob Augustine was what you would call an exceedingly good-looking chap, about six feet two inches tall, slender, about 35 years old, and, as he had spent half of his life in the saddle, a slight bow-leggedness could be noticed. He walked erect with a nonchalant demeanor. He always wore a large ornamented Mexican hat; he had long wavy hair, parted in the middle, it fell gracefully on his broad shoulders; he had a fine chiseled face and a slightly aquiline nose, brown, expressive eyes, eyebrows at least half an inch long, a little black moustache and pearl white teeth. His mouth turned slightly upwards at the corners and often would he smile the smile of a young bashful girl. He was just the type of man that a woman would fall in love with, but back of those eyes lurked the savage. The least thing would arouse his ire and woe to him who got in his path; his bullet would always find its mark.

He always wore an immaculately clean white ruffled shirt and a long red silk necktie, about 15 inches long. He seldom wore a coat, but wore a vest, beautifully embroidered in front and in the back. His trousers were ash gray corduroy. He wore handsome polished boots with leather trimmings with high heels, and he had small feet.

The judge was a queer-looking jigger, and reminded me of an owl and a shrimp. The owl part consisted of his big head, a long hook nose, on which were posed a pair of very large eyeglasses, which always appeared to reflect a glitter; he had broad shoulders, big hips, and when seated his legs were always outstretched, his feet invariably crossed and tapering to a point like a shrimp's tail.

Then there was Bill Lyons, who I believe was chief of police, a man powerfully built, a round face with a black moustache; he certainly was a man of indomitable courage. He knew not what fear was. Mr. Seffel was a policeman, also very tall and exceedingly strong. . . .

Asa Mitchel was Irish, and Peñaloza was a powerful, handsome Mexican about six feet four inches tall, and must have weighed at least 300 pounds. These two men organized the vigilance committee and were the leaders. . . .

The jury that sat in judgment on this case was a very motley crowd. I remember one of them had a suit made of jaguar skin, another one was a tall individual, fine featured, a long goatee, and fierce mutton chops ornamented his face. The majority had long hair and shaggy beards. A few were clean shaven and wore short hair, but all wore their pants in their boots. When they were impaneled as jurors, I am sure they were not sworn in, otherwise I would have remembered this action.

Bob Augustine was a wonderful horseman, and a never-erring marksman. About three months prior to his undoing, he gave an exhibition of his marksmanship on the Alameda [East Commerce

Street] near where now is the Southern Pacific depot. With a six shooter in each hand, afoot, he would blaze away, and without looking would plant a bullet in the center of a different mesquite tree, then he would repeat this mounted on a galloping horse, never scoring a miss out of at least 100 shots.

Everybody knew Bob was a dangerous man to tackle; nevertheless the Vigilantes kept an eye on him. He behaved well for some time, but all of a sudden he could not resist the temptation. He went over to the San Pedro district, got drunk, yelled, shot out lights, shot at door knobs and shot a man through the leg. Mounted on his horse, he rode up to Military Plaza, gave out a terrific howl, charged the chili stands, knocked the tables over. Dismounting, he chased the screaming chili queens and scattered them in every direction. Bill Lyons hurried over, grabbed him by his long hair and locked him in the Bat Cave. It was about 8 o'clock in the evening.

The news spread like wildfire. Everybody was told the Vigilantes would get him and hang him in the morning. Of course I and many boys played hookey, which meant for me a flogging the following day. I squeezed myself through the crowd into the courtroom.

The judge was sitting in a corner, with outstretched legs, smoking his pipe. In the center of the room stood a long table, about six feet wide and 12 feet long, covered with a green smooth cloth like a billiard table. Later on I figured it out that after court was held some lively gambling would be indulged in.

Judge: "Officer, bring in Bob Augustine." Bob appeared with his sombrero under his arm and sat opposite the judge.

Judge: "Good morning, Bob! Bob, I see you have played h--- again and I am going to render judgment. Are you guilty or not guilty?"

Bob: "I refuse to answer."

Judge: "I repeat, are you guilty or not guilty?" At this Bob looked daggers at the judge and said, "It is for you to find out, what are you here for anyway," and with an oath and with a blow of the fist on the table Bob said: "Judge, I want you to understand that I am a free-born Texan and I demand a jury."

The judge appeared fidgety and repeatedly recrossed his legs. He said: "Officer, go out there and bring twelve men to act as a jury."

After a delay of about half an hour, twelve men appeared, the judge bade them be seated. One of the jurors said, "Judge, there are only four chairs in here." The judge shouted at the officer, "What became of them chairs?"

Well, the explanation was the Mexicans had a baile [ball] at San Pedro Park. They borrowed them and had not yet returned them. One of the jurors was resourceful and said, "Let us go over to Moke's and get some boxes."

After they were all seated the judge said, "Now, you fellows are to decide whether Bob Augustine is guilty or not guilty. He will not plead either way and we have our witnesses and Bob can get his---" and here the judge was interrupted by Bob with a wave of the hand, "Judge, hold your trap a minute. I want to have a look at this jury."

And with this he folded his arms, leisurely looked every man square in the eyes, at his discomfort, scanned him from head to foot, and when he got about halfway through said, "Men, I'm taking a photograph of you, I want your faces so impressed on my brain that I shall not forget, and if you convict me I'll get out of jail, and as sure as I am sitting on this chair, I will make every one of you bite the dust," and pointing his finger at the judge said, "and this counts for you too, Judge."

The judge fidgeted and the jurymen looked amazed at each other, and the proceedings were interrupted for some time. One juror asked the judge to come over. They gathered in a bunch, and after a delay of about half an hour the judge stepped forward and said:

"Bob, we have had a preliminary consultation in regard to your doings, and we have come to the conclusion that you are not guilty. It is true, you shot out lights, shot at door knobs, and shot a man in the leg, but you didn't kill anybody, and the one whom we blame is the fellow who sold you that rotten whiskey, and if I had him right here, I would help hang him, wouldn't you, jury?" Of course they all assented. The judge turned towards Bob and said, "You are now discharged and you can go."

Bob: "Judge, I want to thank you and also the jury and I want you to fork over them two sixshooters of mine."

The Judge answered, "Bob, you can have them, but there will not be any cartridges in them. Two rangers will see you ten miles north of San Antonio, and the next place where you can buy your cartridges will be at New Braunfels."

Bob: "Judge, this is not treating me fair."

Judge: "Under the circumstances, it is fair enough."

While all this was going on, Vigilantes, about 300 men, gathered on the south side of Military Plaza. Bob had not noticed them, but all of sudden he stood still, visibly affected, and he said, "Judge, put me back in jail, I don't like the looks of yonder men out there."

But the judge refused to put him back. Bob showed nervousness. He paced up and down and curiosity led him to put his head out of the window to look at the crowd, when Fritz Schreiner and another man pounced upon him, grabbed him by his long hair and yanked him out of the window. The waiting crowd gave a yell, and rushed forward shouting: "Hang him! Hang him!"

In all my life I have never heard a human being bellow as did Bob Augustine. He pleaded in vain. "Please don't hang me, please don't, do it out of consideration for my mother, what will she say when she hears her Bob was strung up with a rope? Please don't hang me. Shoot me, I'll stand up like a man, please."

Just then someone tapped him on the head with a sixshooter saying, "Shut up you varmint." For a few moments he stopped bellowing.

Somebody said, "Let's hang him on a China tree in front of the Bishop's house." The crowd rushed him under one of the trees, tied his hands back of him, his legs were free, then Bob commenced bellowing again. All this commotion brought out the Bishop. On his knees he begged them not to hang him in front of this sanctified building. The crowd cursed him; the Bishop arose, held his hands heavenward and said, "Almighty God, forgive these men for they know not what they're doing, forgive them."

He walked calmly towards the building, ignoring taunts and insults, opened the door and disappeared. Bob, in the meantime, was still bellowing and begging for mercy. Someone shouted: "We want a volunteer with a good horse to pull him up," and instead of one or two coming forward, there were at least 20 who wanted the job.

The noose was adjusted, no cap was used to hide his face, the rope was thrown over a strong limb, the horseman tied the rope to

the pommel of the saddle, when suddenly a Frenchman by the name of Poinsard interrupted the proceedings, wabbled forward and said:

"Wiz ze parmission of ze men I vood like to say a very few words to Bob Augustine."

He stepped in front of him and said, "Meestaire Bob Augustine, you probably do not remember me. I am Mistaire Poinsard. I am a Frenchman, who loves his wine and beer. You know ze Bull's Head Sahloon on Marquette Street, I entered ze sahloon and I step-ped up to ze countaire and I said, 'Bartendaire, give me a glass of beer,' and you turn-ned around and you said, 'Vot ze----you vant in here,' and I said 'Meester Bob, remembaire zis is a free countree,' but you said, 'to ---- viz ze free countree,' and you tok your peestle and you hit me in ze mouze and" (pointing to his mouth) "deeze teeze you knock-ked out.

"I fell on ze floor, you abussed me and kick-ked me in the vairy abominable mannaire and I stayed in bed 10 days, but ze objecte of my viseete is siz: I come here to forgive you for ze abuse you have perpertrated upon me, and ven I say I forgive you, I mean diz viz all my heart and soul and" (holding hands aloft) "I call upon my God to vitnesse da vot I say I meen eet. I forgeeve you for what you have done to me in zis world, but Bob, you have a vairy long voyahge to take, and I don't know vot St. Petaire vill do at the odder end. So I say good-by, Bob, zat is all I vant to say."

For a while the crowd appeared nonplused, but a man shouted "yank him up."

Well, Bob went up and I stood within 20 feet and saw it all. It was terrible to behold. It was so disgustingly fascinating. I stood there trembling all over, but could not take my eyes from him. His eyes bulged out, his tongue came out, and I imagined as everybody else did, that his eyes were fixed on each one.

When the death struggle came, there was a heaving of the breast, his legs spread out convulsively and something cracked as though his bones were breaking. It made such a terrible impression upon me that, for at least four months, I would not sleep by myself; I always slept with an older brother. Generally when a hanging took place the body or bodies were left there until after school hours, for the benefit of the pupils.

I and a friend of mine, Paul Sauer, who is still alive, went there in the afternoon, and found four more men hanging there on the same tree. Lanky Pete was a prestamo man who would force a loan at the point of a bowie knife. A man had been stabbed in the heart on Cameron (Crawfish) Street. The knife was found sticking in his heart, with the name of Lanky Pete on it.

At the corner of South Flores and Military Plaza, four more men were hanging. They were strung up on general principles. Another man, a notorious horse thief, was hanging on a gigantic pecan tree, back of Stumberg's store and campyard, corner of Nueva and South Flores Streets.

After I got home from Bob's hanging I got a good flogging for going to the hanging, the next day I got another flogging for having played hookey. On this same day, the Bishop had 10 beautiful China trees cut down, for fear there might be another hanging, and as he said, it pained him very much to see men hanging right at his door and it never happened again.

— Charles A. Herff, *San Antonio Express*, January 22, 1928

9.
Gaming Tables

The tearing down recently of the old Jack Harris vaudeville theater and gambling house and the more recent destruction of the block of buildings in which the Silver King former gambling resort is located—and this historic structure is also doomed—recalls the days when gaming was at its acme and flourished here. . . .

The first places where gaming was conducted were out in the open on the plazas, but principally on Main Plaza, the center of which was for many years—nearly two centuries—reserved for sports of all sorts, but principally various games of chance at cards, notably "monte," the favorite game here for years. . . .

Not only the men but the women gambled openly and, as a rule, the games were fair. In fact, short shrift generally was the fate of any one caught cheating during any of the deals. Not only the governors and other high public officials, but the grand dames of their families, gathered around the "lay-outs" and staked their money on their favorite cards. The betting was high, sometimes almost reaching to the wide-open sky above. The only limit was the store of the games or that of the players. . . .

The tables or other furniture used for the games were arranged about a quadrangle on the plaza, allowing sufficient space for the vehicles and other traffic to have passage way. These tables were ornamented with various devices to attract the attention of players. The play went on during the day and night.

While some games opened in the morning and had some attention from the sportively inclined, most opened in the afternoon after everyone had indulged in his or her siesta, or midday nap. This was usually after 3 p.m. But it was at night that the play was at its height and the crowd the greatest. Games then were rarely conducted indoors unless the weather was too inclement. The wind had to be strong enough to blow the cards away or the rain hard enough to wet them so the dealers could not shuffle or deal.

Of course there were private games among the prominent social groups, and these took place in the dwellings of the players, but even the puissant politicians and officials preferred the al fresco play. Refreshments were always handy at night on all of the plazas, but particularly in the immediate vicinity of the gaming. "Fondas" were vended, the various viands popular among the players and populace in general were scattered about the plazas.

The open-air play continued as long as the dominion of the Spanish . . . and the Mexicans lasted. When the Texas Republic was established the play was relegated to places that were roofed and more sheltered as well as more sequestered. It was not a penal offense until after the establishment of the Texas Republic. It is still conducted in the open air in Mexico, where the officials from the President down to the peons indulge in the hazards. When it became an offense against the law in San Antonio, this fact did not prevent the populace from playing. The penalty at first was merely a fine, and of not a very heavy amount.

Even then it was not considered improper gambling. The merchants, the lawyers, the judges and the jurors, as well as the doctors, "bucked" against the different games. The records show that several of the sheriffs, mayors and other prominent people pleaded guilty and paid their nominal fines. Public gaming on the ground floor continued throughout the days of the Republic and during the dominion of the State until about 30 years ago, when a stringent city ordinance was adopted, prohibiting it on the ground floor, and it was then conducted on the upper floors until it was finally suppressed by the adoption of a stricter penal statute. . . .

Never at any time has the social standing, prestige or popularity of any person suffered on account of participating in gambling. It has never affected the eligibility of any public official or private individual as long as such person dealt or played fairly. . . . Not only has a propensity to indulge in such sport not affected the reputation or standing of private citizens or public officials, but there have been and there are still here men who have been professional gamblers whose probity has never been questioned. Their lives, outside of their sporting proclivities, have compared very favorably with those who have played against their games. Those living here still are honored and respected. Those who are dead are still mourned and spoken of with reverence whenever their names are mentioned. All of them are known never to have turned a crooked card or dealt any other than a square deal. Frequently flowers are placed on their graves, although, in one instance, a generation or more may have elapsed since they finally "cashed in."

In the days when gambling was at its zenith here, which was along in the period immediately preceding and during the Civil War, or just after its close, many fortunes were won and lost. The winnings were principally by gamblers conducting the games and not by the players, but there were some exceptions, and several players won and in some instances broke the game. This was notably so in the instance of an army officer who had made a specialty of "chuck-a-luck" as well as poker.

Entering a gambling establishment, he got into a poker game and soon saw he stood no show to win and drew out. He then made a proposition to the gambler conducting the "chuck-a-luck" game to play it without a limit if the gambler would play it square. At first he did not play very heavily, but, seeing that he was getting a fair play, he began to increase his stakes. In a few plays by doubling them he broke the game, which the dealer was compelled to close.

All gambling resorts had saloons in connection. Some had variety shows and dance halls operating in combination. All were money makers for the owners and separators for the players, customers and patrons, although most gambling establishments were conducted fairly. Probably the most noted was that known as the Old Bull's Head. This had a saloon in connection, but no theatrical or terpsichorean adjunct. It had its inception about the beginning of the days of the Republic and was located in an alley east of the old Market House, at the corner of Market and Yturri Streets.

Here, as in the other establishments of early days, money was displayed so profusely and abundantly that it can best be described by a phrase used by one of the old-time gamblers who said:

"It was in heaps and heaps—in piles and stacks. It towered high on the tops of the tables and was often handled with shovel like scoops. The greatest quantity was of silver, principally of the denomination of 'dobe, or Mexican dollars, and halves, although tall stacks of $50, $20, $10 and $5 gold pieces as well as Spanish doubloons stood in the middle of the tables or on them beside the bets of the players. These coins jingled as they were nimbly juggled by the deft fingers of the dealers or the 'look-outs,' as the men employed by the 'house' to watch over the games, were called, and who paid all bets won by the players or raked in all bets lost by the latter."

The money of the players was not only carried in "morals," or bags, to the tables by the players or their servants, but sometimes it was hauled to gambling houses in Mexican oxcarts or "carretas" or in other vehicles. But money was not the only thing wagered. Many old stockmen played not only their small numbers of cattle or staked single steers but sometimes whole herds of hoofed animals, both cattle and horses, goats and sheep, oxen or mules and wagons.

In the slavery days . . . [slaves] were staked on the results of the cards. The value of such "stakes" ranged all the way from a few hundred to several thousand dollars. Some of those slaves who constituted such wagers are still living in San Antonio. They were the property until the emancipation proclamation of some of the prominent people here. Several are still living in the families of those who either won them or lost them. Some who were lost by their owners and won by the dealers went back to their former owners who had bet and lost them. Some, but very few, stayed with the gamblers, who either sold them or lost them in other games.

Generally the play at the various games was conducted in strictest silence and without interruption, except the games of roulette, "Keno" and the much more modern one of "craps," during the progress of which the dealers called the winning numbers. As these were called, the players vociferated with various expletives expressive of their feeling and indicative of their luck or its lack.

Sometimes, however, the silence of the play was rudely shattered and punctuated with poinards or bowie knives, pistols and other weapons and death of one or more persons resulted while their forms as well as the hands of those who slew them, the cards and tables, the floors and the walls were crimsoned with the blood of those who had been so rash as to use intemperate speeches of implication or innuendo. Such instances were not of infrequent occurrence at the Old Bull's Head, or in its immediate environment, particularly in the two alleyways on which it stood, and in the Market House west of it.

Some of these tragedies were particularly thrilling. One involved the extermination of an entire family and their unfaithful servant as well as killing of some of those concerned in the murder of this family, which was an old Spanish one.

Because of the unsettled condition here, it was concluded to return to Spain. The men possessed a large number of Spanish doubloons, which were placed in leather bags and put in the ambulance in which the family started, accompanied by their faithless servant, who was the driver. This man was in league with three gamblers, whom he informed of the family's intentions, and who murdered them and took the gold which the servant helped to place on their horses. He returned with them on one of the horses.

The robbers, who were frequenters of the Bull's Head, went there and left the servant outside with the gold until they could ascertain if the way was clear to one of the rear rooms into which they were to take the loot and divide it. The servant, while they were gone, threw the largest bag of gold into a well, thinking that he was unseen and that the bag would not be missed when the gamblers returned, as they did soon after.

Missing that bag of gold, they did not parlay with the servant when the latter denied taking the money. They promptly stabbed him through the heart and took the remaining money into the room. There they disagreed over the division and in the quarrel two of the three were killed. The other escaped with the money and was never heard of after.

The hiding of the money was witnessed by a person who had a small establishment facing on this alley and not far from the well. He also saw the killing of the servant. He discreetly waited until the corpses of the servant and the two gamblers had been buried. He was even particular to see that the lids of the coffins had been nailed down securely, and it is even stated he was the only person, except the man who drove the cart carrying the corpses, to accompany the bodies to the grave.

Then he waited until he got a chance to remove unobserved the money from the well. It was a considerable sum and enriched him sufficiently to purchase valuable property and take a trip to Europe. He stated he had inherited the money from a wealthy relative who had died in a foreign land. . . .

Another instance occurred soon after the success of the Republic against Mexico. The sum of $50,000 was sent here for distribution among Mexicans to foment a revolution against the young Republic. Those to whom it was addressed were indiscreet. They played against some of the games in the Old Bull's Head and lost a small portion, but the gamblers were not satisfied with winning that and, fearing that a considerable portion might be applied to the intended purpose, and learning of the whereabouts of the money, stole it and got away with it.

One of the persons who had great wealth and was wont to wager it liberally at the Bull's Head was a grandee known as Don Diego de Talamantes. On one occasion, after making a fair winning he staked a gambler who was broke and wanted to open a game there. Some of the other gamblers, who found out the Don had much money and that he was going to leave here with it, determined to rob and murder him when he had proceeded a short distance from the city. He was to travel in an ambulance. The gambler he staked found out the plan of the other gamblers and proposed with them to take part. His motive was to save the Don's life. He agreed to be the one to shoot the Don while they were to shoot his driver and servant.

He told the Don and the Sheriff. The latter and some of his deputies hid near the place where the attack was proposed. The robbers, however, changed their plans and attacked at another point nearer the city. They killed the Don's driver and servant, but the gambler friend shot both of the other gamblers, killing one and wounding the other. He helped the Don to overpower and fetter the wounded man until the Sheriff could be notified and come after him. The wounded gambler died soon after reaching the city. The Don's friend was exonerated.

It would have been better for the Don if he remained steadfast in his purpose to take his money away. But he returned to the Bull's Head where he lost all of it, and his ambulance and team of horses. His friend, whom he had staked, won a considerable portion of it, but it was distributed around among most of the other gamblers. . .

The Don had won the smiles and favors of a dark-eyed senorita, but when he went broke she had no more smiles or favors for him. The successful gambler, whom the Don had staked, succeeded to her smiles and favors, and even let the aristocrat have money enough to get out of town with, buying him a horse, bridle and saddle and handing him a neat sum in cash. The Don never came back.

Near the old Bull's Head and Market House was a hotel kept by a man named McLain. One night a row between two Mexicans started in the Bull's Head and continued in the street. McLain tried to separate the belligerents and met the fate of most peacemakers. He was killed, as were both of the fighters. A woman bullfighter, known as "Tambora," or "the drum," probably because she beat the drum in the bullfight parades, was among those who were killed in the vicinity while seated at one of the games. The shot was fired from someone outside whose identity was never learned. . . .

In the immediate vicinity there was a gambling establishment conducted in the third story of the building at the northeast corner of Main Plaza and Market Street, where the Prudential Insurance Building now stands. It was first called "The Banner," and finally "The Clipper." There was another on Dolorosa Street known as "The Ranch," upstairs above the southeast corner of that thoroughfare and Military Plaza, or North Flores Street, and still another, the name of which has been forgotten, located in the center of the block now occupied by the Southern Hotel, but long before the latter caravansary was built.

On the corner of Main Plaza and Soledad Street was the old Jack Harris combined vaudeville theater, saloon and gambling house, whose history is very familiar and has recently been fully published by *The Express*, making it unnecessary to detail it in this story. Adjoining it in the old Plaza House, "Rowdy Joe" Lowe, Kate Lowe and Joel Collins conducted a combined variety theater, saloon and gambling house.

Next to the Old Plaza House was the Crystal saloon and gambling house. Adjoining it was an establishment known as the White Elephant. Probably it took its title from the fact that the tiger could be tackled there by those to whom their money was a white elephant, or possibly to distinguish it from a similar establishment known as the Black Elephant, which had preceded it by several generations. This latter, a saloon and gaming place, was located at the northwest corner of West Nueva and South Flores Street.

In the middle of the block on South Flores between Military Plaza and Nueva Streets was another gaming establishment whose name is not remembered, although some of the incidents that happened there are recalled. At the corner of Military Plaza and Trevino Street on the north side of the latter was a sporting establishment known as the Arlington. In a place known as the Blue Front, a gambling house and variety theater, one of the famous tragedies of sporting circles took place when one of the actresses, Georgia Drake, probably one of the most beautiful women who ever came to this city, was killed and a soldier badly wounded at the same time.

There were a couple of gambling houses on Main Avenue at the time that thoroughfare was called Acequia Street. They were in the vicinity of Houston Street. The Silver King was probably the latest public gambling house to be established here and the last to be torn down. It succeeded the gambling house that had been previously conducted at the Fashion theater on the west side of Military Plaza. At one time there was a gambling house on Houston Street adjoining the southeast corner of that street and North Flores Street. A place kept by Tom Comerford called the Occident was also located on the west side of Military Plaza.

Besides these were several on the other side of "The Creek" or in the trans-San Pedro [Creek] district. Most prominent among these were the Star on the north side of Commerce Street midway between the creek and Laredo Street, the Washington at the northeast corner of Laredo and Commerce Street, the Grey Mule, for negroes, at the northwest corner of those thoroughfares, and the Bella Union at the northeast corner of Dolorosa and Laredo Streets.

— *San Antonio Express*, January 31, 1915

10.
Chapel of the Miracles

In the triangle formed by Laredo, Ruiz and Salado streets and on Ruiz Street is a quaint structure that, although famous, attracts but little attention from the ordinary passerby. It is in such an isolated neighborhood that very few ever visit it, and yet there are many who make long pilgrimages to do so.

The place is a small private Catholic chapel. Its name is "Our Saviour of Miracles" or "Nuestro Sr. de los Milagros," as the inscription on the cross above it indicates. On the other side of the cross is the inscription . . . [which] indicates that it was built in 1813, but this is likely to be an error as the history of the chapel, which is authentic, and its main feature, differ in dates. The chapel was erected to shelter a statue that is much more famous than any other feature and forms the main object of the shrine.

This statue itself has a very interesting history. It was brought to this country from Spain by the Franciscan Friars about 1716 and placed originally in San Fernando Cathedral. There it remained for some years until a fire consumed a considerable portion of this edifice. It was rescued from this fire and carried to one of a row of adobe huts that stood on the north side of the Main Plaza about where the present Bexar County courthouse is.

This was the first fire in the Old Cathedral of San Fernando. There was another fire just about the time of the Civil War, or shortly before hostilities broke out. The latter fire destroyed all but the rear portion. The old walls were adobe, having been replaced by solid stone walls and two towers having superceded the single one that stood on the west side of the Main Plaza, while the rear or unburned portion was on the east side of Military Plaza.

The family whose members saved this sacred relic from the flames of the first fire were named Jimenez. After they rescued it, they retained it and built a shrine for its reception. They had heard of its miraculous efficacy. It had been famous in Spain before being brought hither. The Franciscans had brought it here for the purpose of converting the Indians and for use in teaching them the lessons of Catholicism. The savages saw the statue, heard the words of the Friars, and were converted in large numbers. Not a few became devout members of the church.

Then came the fire which encompassed the partial destruction of the cathedral and some of the statues placed there. This one was saved and carried to the first place mentioned. After it was set up there, the priests would not recognize the shrine nor say masses there, and for a long time placed it under the ban. Later on the Jimenez family removed it.

Old Don Juan Jimenez, who died here about five years ago almost a centenarian, received it from his elder brother, who built the chapel at 113 Ruiz Street, where it now is enshrined. He bequeathed it as his most precious possession to his daughter Candelaria, who is now the wife of Clemente Rodriguez. The chapel is on the same premises as her house. A large double gate admits to both. The chapel has a broad portal. Above this is painted a pair of outstretched wings and the cross is above them.

There are always devotees within it whenever it is open. These are ever to be found kneeling and reciting some orison. They invariably kneel before this statue, which is suspended in the center of the eastern end of the edifice. The statue itself is the object that engages and commands continuous attention. It was an ancient object at the time it was brought hither from Spain. The statue is a representation of Our Savior on the Cross. About it is a pale blue tunic. This tunic is a garment that is greatly venerated. The chapel, the statue, and the tunic are much more famous elsewhere than here. Their fame is extant over Mexico and many have come all the way from there to offer orisons before the statue and within the chapel.

Those who come there to pray invariably make an offering promising if their supplications are heeded and their prayers granted

to give some valuable object. Most of the supplicants are those who are afflicted with some malady. The offerings they give are generally representative of the part afflicted. The votive offerings are invariably of either silver or of gold according to the means of the afflicted supplicants. Most of these offerings, which are miniature hands, arms, or various limbs, are pinned to the tunic about the statue. Their prayers do not always relate to the supplicants themselves, but sometimes to their possessions. For this reason several miniature horses and dogs or other animals are to be seen there.

One of the supplicants who gave a votive offering was a wealthy widow residing in Mexico. She suffered from some painful malady of the head and her offering was a crown of thorns. The thorns were of gold and their base or support was silver. This offering was very expensive. She spent some time in prayer before this statue, after which she returned to her Mexican home from whence she came all the way here to make her devotions at this shrine. On her return she had the offering made by a jeweler there and sent it here by express.

Most of those who go there to pray carry a candle with them and kneel and pray as long as the candle burns. They carry a fresh candle with them each time they visit the place. Sometimes there are several supplicants there. All of them are earnest and devout. They never interfere with each other or notice one another.

This chapel is one of the places where the famous play of the Pastores is held. This is usually during Advent and up to Christmas Eve. Sometimes the play is prolonged until after the New Year begins. These productions of the Pastores do not seem to interrupt the devotions of those supplicate before it. They either join the players or resume their orisons after the players have finished their performances.

When the Pastores are being produced there the chapel is decorated especially for the latter occasion. On general occasions it has other decorations besides the statue mentioned. These decorations consist principally of pictures of members of the Holy Family, but there are also flowers and other ornaments about the place. At each side of the chapel are wooden settees placed there to seat those who are not kneeling in supplication. The latter kneel on the hard, bare floor. They also are true to their promises. They invariably keep them and present the gift they offer at the commencement of their supplications. No one is ever known to have failed to keep faith.

Many miracles are alleged to have been the result of the prayers offered at this shrine and by those kneeling before this statue. Some evidences of them have been left in the chapel as mute witnesses. These evidences are rude crutches of the halt and lame who, having been cured, left their crutches behind to attest their cures. Many tourists, actuated by no other impulse than curiosity, visit this chapel. They allude to it as the "Wonder Chapel." Some of them find it interesting and fee the people who own it. Others merely glance at it and go on . . . .

I have never heard of any of the other statues being venerated as that in the little chapel on Ruiz Street. This latter seems to be the most famous statue in San Antonio. It is likely that it is older than any of those even now in San Fernando Cathedral. It appears to be about 3 1/2 feet tall. Although apparently fragile, it has stood through several centuries the strains of time but has received great care, which doubtless accounts for its almost miraculous preservation. The fabric about it seems frail also, but it continues to hold the objects suspended from it and doubtless contains strength with its ornamentality.

Until very recently the old chapel on Ruiz Street was in a very dilapidated condition. Its walls showed evidences of decay and it otherwise gave visible evidence of the carking tooth of time.

But recently some mysterious and anonymous friend, probably one of the supplicants, supplied funds for its repair, and its appearance has considerably changed. The old walls have been painted up, their crevices filled and a new coat of whitewash has been given the outside. Inside, new woodwork has been placed to form the interior walls, fresh paint enlivens the chapel and the ornaments have been brightened so that the place has not the same aged appearance it had a few years ago, but the statue still appears as of old, but bearing little evidence of the great age it has attained.

— Charles Merritt Barnes, *San Antonio Express*, April 28, 1907

11.

Campo Santo—Holy Ground

In 1738 the Canary Islanders began the building of the San Fernando Cathedral. With the growth of a handful of Spaniards, who were not the helpers of the priests about the missions, there arose the need for a civic cemetery, and around the parish church, where the cathedral now stands, the first graves of the new burying ground were placed.

"Campo Santo," Holy Ground, this plot about the church was called by the Canary Islanders whose burial ground it became. The bodies placed there were never moved, though today no stones designate them and here again people passing busily about the City Hall or the Courthouse do not know that they pass the graves of the makers of the local government which they are only continuing.

The ground around the cathedral, now Main Plaza, was called then "Plaza de las Islas," . . . and this oldest civic burial ground in San Antonio became known as the Canary Island Cemetery. . . . Of the first group of Spaniards who settled about the old cathedral, all were buried in the "Campo Santo" except the last, Catarina Leal, who died in 1808 and was buried in the new San Antonio Cemetery, which had been founded in that year, where the Santa Rosa Hospital now stands.

Within the old cathedral are other graves, these still marked by marble slabs upon which some index to the past may still be found. Traditions, too, have grown up about the graves within the cathedral, and there are many who believe that the charred bones of the Alamo victims rest within these old vaults. Here is the grave of Ignacio Elizondo, colonel of calvary, who betrayed to their death

the Mexican troops with whom he had fought in the first revolt from Spain. And here also is the grave of Eugenio Navarro, whose name is forever linked with the San Fernando Cathedral through the gifts that he made to it.

In those days, while his older brother, Col. José Navarro, helped the Texans fight for their freedom from Mexico, Eugenio looked well to his caravans of mules that passed regularly from San Antonio to New Orleans. And on one trip he charged his men with the bringing of a valuable and mysterious package that would await them there. Arriving finally in San Antonio, the package was found to contain cathedral bells, brought from Europe by order of Navarro and guarded by his men carefully through the hundreds of unmapped miles between New Orleans and San Antonio.

Afterward, in defending the honor of a friend, Eugenio Navarro was killed—not before he had stabbed to the heart his assailant— and his body was laid in a vault of the cathedral in which he had worshipped. This vault with its quaint inscription and the other graves found here, among them that of Don Manuel Muñoz, first Governor of Texas when it became a separate province of Mexico, who was buried here in 1799, form the oldest group of marked graves to be found in San Antonio.

Next in age to the Campo Santo, or the old Canary Island Cemetery, was the San Antonio Cemetery, which lay where the Santa Rosa Hospital now stands. The first grave placed here was that of the Corsican, José Angel Navarro, uncle of Eugenio Navarro, donor of the cathedral bells, buried in 1808 near the entrance to the new graveyard, in compliance with the request that his body might be placed where all who entered would tread upon his grave. Strange wish, indeed, fulfilled by thousands who have passed above the grave in the century it has lain undisturbed. For though no stone now marks it, the grave was left near the entrance when the burial ground was abandoned and the hospital built there.

According to a custom of the Catholic Church in Europe, burying grounds are not kept up after all the space in them is used. Instead, the stones are removed and the ground given to some charitable work school, church or hospital. So it was with the old San Antonio Cemetery. Many bodies lying there were removed to the

San Fernando Cemetery, others left untouched. No sign of them remains today. Yet among San Antonians are those who can remember when this cemetery lay so far out of town that processions to it were attended by armed, vigilant men. For the Apache and Comanche Indians, sworn enemies of the town long after it passed from Spaniards to Americans, loved to swoop down when inhabitants were gathered unawares at the cemetery beyond the square.

Apart from the Catholic graves of the old San Antonio Cemetery, where Milam Square now stands, the first Protestant settlers were buried. It was here that the body of Ben Milam was placed after its removal from the old Veramendi house where he fell, and here that Capt. Lysander Wells, hero of the battle of San Jacinto, was buried. His grave is unmarked today and only the simple stone, bearing the words of Ben Milam's immortal challenge, indicates the first Protestant burial plot in San Antonio.

The second group of Protestant graves was placed beyond the Alamo along Alameda, "promenade of trees." It is here that some believe the martyrs of the Alamo were buried. Traditions and authorities vary on this point, while all trace of the graves has disappeared. Only the traffic on East Commerce Street marks the ground where the early Protestant settlers of San Antonio, if not its first, dead in the struggle for independence, are buried.

In 1854, San Fernando Cemetery, oldest of the city's present cemeteries, was opened. In it are buried veterans of the Texas Revolution, early settlers and Indian fighters. Among these no grave has greater historic interest than that of Col. José Navarro, writer of the Texas Declaration of Independence and brother of Eugenio Navarro whose body lies in the old San Fernando Cathedral.

Long before the revolution Navarro represented Texas and Coahuila in the Mexican Congress, but, becoming dissatisfied with the oppressive government of Mexico, he threw his lot with the colonists who had begun their struggle for independence, risking all with their fortune. In 1841 he was a member of the ill-fated Santa Fe expedition, in which he was captured and sentenced to death. This decree was changed to one of life imprisonment in the famous political dungeon of Castillo de San Juan, the Bastille of Mexico, on the coast of Vera Cruz.

But through the changing government that characterized Mexico in those days, as in the present, Colonel Navarro obtained his release and returned to serve the Republic he had helped to establish. The busy street in this city and the county in East Texas, both bearing his name, help, as does the stone in San Fernando Cathedral, to perpetuate the name that played so prominent a part in the early history of Texas.

In San Fernando Cemetery also is the grave of John Twohig, banker and famous host, in whose house, La Casa del Rio, were entertained warriors and rulers. Sam Houston, Zachary Taylor, Robert E. Lee and General Grant—all these were his guests in the old Spanish house by the river. In San Fernando, too, is found the grave of Don Antonio Menchaca, who fought in the battle of San Jacinto, and of Don Francisco Ruiz, signer as was Navarro, of the Declaration of Independence and as alcalde of San Antonio during the revolution, said to have buried the dead of the Alamo. Here, too, is the grave of Bryan Callaghan, long mayor of San Antonio.

In the Maverick burial lot east of town is the grave of Sam Maverick, Indian fighter and scout who, with Deaf Smith, helped Milam lead the men who first wrestled San Antonio from the Mexicans. And in the Government Cemetery established in 1847 are buried the veterans of the Mexican War of 1848 and of the Civil War.

Scattered as they are about the city, these burial grounds hold the graves that make San Antonio forever a mecca to those who hold sacred the memory of the soldiers of Texas and the veterans of its wars.

— *San Antonio Express*, August 1, 1920

Part II
The Ladies

Men dominated organized social events in nineteenth-century San Antonio, but by 1900 the ladies had begun to play active roles in the social and civic life of the city. While the "New Woman" could not be found in such large numbers as on the Eastern Seaboard, she had begun to make her presence known. Marin B. Fenwick would be her champion for nearly four decades.

From the early 1890s when Miss Fenwick began to write in the columns of the *Express*, she wrote about the "ladies." The praiseworthy qualities of her ladies, however, coincided with the adjectives commonly ascribed to the "New Woman"—intelligent, knowledgeable, talented and active outside the home. Omnipresent as she was at the major social affairs of this generation, she used her weekly Sunday column to encourage, even propagandize, those goals she regarded as having priority for women—legal and voting rights, higher education, the woman's club movement and leadership in diverse areas of civic and social life. In all these endeavors she enjoyed the patronage of Eleanor Brackenridge, whose bachelor brother George was not only the wealthiest but one of the most philanthropic men in the city.

Miss Fenwick wrote the story about army brides. Settings in which young women accepted their traditional roles by acknowledging social proprieties, but which could also be in juxtaposition with their "abilities to bear hardships and dangers," delighted Miss Fenwick and her readers.

In a somewhat similar vein, Miss Fenwick presented the ladies who founded the Battle of Flowers parade as pioneers. Local business leaders were astounded that the city's most respectable ladies could organize such an endeavor. That it added so much to the local economy delighted downtown merchants.

Hardly any cultural advancement of the early twentieth century could be mentioned without acknowledging feminine leadership. The construction of a public library was regarded as a monumental achievement, and the long struggle of the ladies toward that goal received popular acclaim. In a wholly unrelated area, and one that would make an impact on the entire state of Texas, the creative imagination and persistent leadership of Mrs. John K. Beretta in the preservation of the bluebonnets represented a singular achievement.

Male jocularity reached new heights as American newsmen reported on women's activities outside the home. Doubtless a young bachelor gleefully conjured up the dialogue of the young ladies who planned the leap year party. If such a planning session occurred in reality, it may well have been the first experience these young socialites had in organizing and effecting any sort of gathering.

12.

Mother-in-Law of the Army

Some Cupids kill with arrows, some with traps, "and more are blinded by the glitter of brass buttons and gold lace." The little god of love follows in the wake of the army, and he has a "corking" time when the drums are beating, flags flying and the note of real war is in the air.

There is not an army post in the country that has not had its romance. Even when the soldier is on his lonely bivouac he is receiving absent treatment from some "control" that enables him to endure hardships and dangers and dream of the happy days to come. So completely has Cupid cast his spell over Fort Sam Houston that San Antonio has long been known as the mother-in-law of the army. In the early days the beautiful winding river, the sunny skies and soft breezes gave to this frontier Mexican town the atmosphere that lends itself to love and romance.

Was it strange that Uncle Sam's boys in blue, far from home and friends, fell an easy prey to the bright-eyed maidens that laughed and chatted as they strolled along the banks of the rippling acequias or trained flowers in the patios and petted the gay plumaged birds that hung in gilded wicker cages? Microbes and "lungers" had not yet arrived, neither had the conventionalities of society. Horseback rides across the flower-decked prairies, picnics to the missions, boating parties, when all joined in singing the old songs, accompanied by the sweet notes of the guitar, were some of the traps Cupid laid to ensnare the unwary.

There is no "rest cure" for society when a military wedding is on the tapis. The peace commission has not yet meddled with that branch of the service. The army brides, in the days before sentiment was eclipsed by silver and cut glass, oftentimes went out to face dangers that would have made their pioneer grandfathers quail.

The old Guilbeau home on South Flores Street has been the scene of more brilliant weddings than any other place in San Antonio except St. Mark's Church. It was here that Anita Dwyer was married to the gallant young Lieutenant Withers. Anita was a typical Irish beauty and was just home from Ireland, polished in all the arts and graces of a finishing school. What wonder that she was the favored companion of Gen. Robert E. Lee and Albert Sidney Johnston on their canters over the wide prairies, for her charms ensnared the heart of many a man. She cast her lot with the army and was destined to an eventful career during the dark days of the Civil War.

Even before the days of "daughters" and "dames," pedigrees and "trees" were at premium, and when the gay Olive Ann Jones was married to the handsome young Lieutenant Washington there was no end of social stir. Olive Ann was not only a leading belle, but her beautiful mother had been the favorite niece of Matthew Vassar, and suggested to her uncle the idea of endowing a woman's college, thus making possible the Vassar girl. Lieutenant Washington was a twig of the same cherry tree as the father of the country, so, in a way, this was a royal alliance.

Kate Whitely was noted for her takin' ways, and it was not expected that her marriage to Edward Norton, one of the leaders of the civilian set, would follow in the beaten track—and it didn't. The wedding took place at the arsenal just at the time the solons over in Austin were having strenuous days with the secession ordinance.

Kate was the true daughter of a United States soldier and she made the most of her opportunity. The rooms were elaborately decorated with old Glory, and instead of the usual wedding march the band played the "Star Spangled Banner," "Yankee Doodle" and "Hail Columbia." Kate Anderson, a niece of Major Anderson of Fort Sumter fame, was one of the bridesmaids. "Everybody" was there, but it was before the days of "mental control" and—poor things—they did not know enough to say, "there is no war, all is peace, all is harmony." Two days later Texas went out of the Union and General Whitely was a prisoner of war.

The "befo' de war" bridegrooms had no worry about securing state rooms and there was no secrecy as to the wedding journey, for the army ambulance was the only mode of conveyance. It usually took four or five days to reach Port Lavaca, where sea trips began.

If you think that Cupid went into mourning or even took a vacation during the days of the Civil War, when there was sorrow and death in many a household, you are mistaken. He sent out joyous vibrations, and the girls were so eager for party togs that they willingly paid $20 per yard Confederate money for tarleton, which was quite as correct as is chiffon today.

There was much social gaiety in San Antonio during that time on account of the continual coming and going to and from Mexico. This, doubtless, led to the marriage of Mary Vanderlip to George Chabot, British consul at San Luis Potosi.

So far as the dangers from war were concerned, Mary was jumping from the frying pan into the fire, for the Maximilian troubles were at their height; soldiers were crowding the streets, fighting and dying. The Chabots were protected by the Union Jack, but were in constant danger from stray bullets. They had, however, many experiences which are more enjoyable to contemplate through the vista of years than they were at the time. Mrs. Chabot often saw the ill-fated Carlotta, who is said to have estranged the warm-hearted natives by her cold and haughty bearing. Mr. and Mrs. Edward Norton were making their way to Europe via Vera Cruz about this time, and they accompanied the Chabots as far as Monterrey on their long overland wedding journey.

General Grant had no more effective ally during the perplexing days of Reconstruction than Cupid. When the United States soldiers came marching back, spic and span, in their new uniforms, the girls decided they would give them a "frost," at least that is what they would have said if they had been "up" on latter day slang. Just how the boycott was broken Cupid only knows, but it was soon noted that "going into the silence" was no longer practiced by the girls, and from that day to this the marriage of Texas girls with United States soldiers has been as common as appendicitis.

One of the first girls to join the army was Delia Vanderlip, who married Lieutenant Cresson. The wedding took place in the First

Presbyterian Church, and even though the bride wore a Paris gown of brocaded satin she went away, like the rest of them, in the army ambulance—but only as far as Columbus, where they took the train to Houston. They made the trip to Philadelphia in ten days, which was record time.

A wedding which was to have been celebrated with every new wrinkle known to the effete East was that of Miss McGavock to Major Whiteside. However, "the best laid plans," etc., there came a spell of weather, the roads were impassable and the bride's wedding outfit was missing. On the wedding day a white satin gown was rushed through by the army tailor. The marriage took place in the old Paschal homestead on Soledad Street, and this was the first time in San Antonio that a house had been darkened for a day function. The roads remained impassable and the bride was compelled to attend many wedding festivities without her bridal accessories.

The marriage of Lieut. Charles Smith to Miss Cassiano was one of the large and brilliant affairs of Reconstruction days.

General Mason, the first commander of the Department of Texas after the war, held a trying position, but he and his charming wife won all hearts. Their daughter Kate married Captain Eckels, the wedding took place at the old Guilbeau House, at the time the general's quarters. This was decidedly the most brilliant army wedding up to that time celebrated in San Antonio. And better than all of the display, was the real feeling of interest and love all felt for the young bride. In this same old house a few years later a large company of friends gathered to witness the marriage of Jennie, daughter of General Auger, to Major Russell.

The "oldest inhabitant" will have no more entertaining story to tell than the romance of the international wedding, which stirred this little town quite as much as Gotham is stirred when a lord comes from over the sea to carry off the daughter of a millionaire. The contracting parties were General Treviño, commander of the Mexican army, and Bertie, the daughter of Gen. E. O. C. Ord, commander of the Department of Texas.

In the unsettled days of the '70s, General Ord had many difficult situations to handle and his clever management of border troubles more than once prevented international war. On one of his trips to the border to hold a conference with the Mexican generals he was accompanied by his daughter, and here she met for the first time General Treviño. The girl was young and fair as a lily and could speak no Spanish; the general was a swarthy warrior and could speak no English. If Cupid laughs at locksmiths he also ignores "tongues," for he knows right well that eyes can look love to eyes.

A few months later General and Mrs. Grant came to Texas and General Treviño and staff came to pay their respects to the old commander. During these festivities the young couple were thrown much together. They were both in the party that went to Galveston to meet the general and escort him to San Antonio. Col. H. B. Andrews' private car Texas was attached to the train, and it had been handsomely decorated in honor of the distinguished guests.

General Ord was prevented from making the trip, much to his regret, for he was one of Grant's most valued commanders. The family was represented by Bertie, who was chaperoned by Mrs. Andrews and shared in the many honors showered upon the visitors. Of course, it is perfectly delightful to be in the swim and know you are on the very crest of the wave. Cupid knows how to delight the heart of a young girl and tickle the vanity of an old warrior.

It was, however, more than a year after this before the marriage was consummated. In the meantime General Treviño made several visits to San Antonio, always bearing beautiful gifts that stirred the heart of the bride and quite turned the heads of all the ambitious young girls of her set.

In May, 1880, General Treviño sent three of his generals to this city to arrange all of the details of the marriage. Two months later it was solemnized in St. Mark's Church, Dean Richardson officiating. A large reception followed at General Ord's quarters, which were in the Gallagher homestead in the rear of the Alamo.

In the days immediately preceding the wedding there was a perfect round of house parties and merrymakings going on at the home of the Ords. The First and the Twenty-fifth regiments of infantry were here, one just going, the other just coming, but both stayed to take part in and add to the splendors of the wedding. Colonel (now General) Maus was among the popular army beaus that quite rivaled the matinee idol with the girls.

General Treviño had with him his staff and a retinue of servants. When they set off on their journey southward, the fair young bride guarded by this company of bronzed soldiers, they might have been mistaken for the retainers of an oriental prince, although instead of palanquin the bride rode in a carriage, and in lieu of sacred banyan groves, peacocks and turtle doves, they had before them the cacti-covered plains, coyotes and jack rabbits.

The army weddings of recent years have been too numerous to chronicle. San Antonio's daughters have followed their soldier husbands to the Philippines, to Alaska, the islands of the sea and in lonely frontier camps and as a rule they have proven themselves fitting companions for brave men.

— Marin B. Fenwick, *San Antonio Express*, May 28, 1911

13.
Fiesta Recollections

Those who participated in the first Flower Battle, 20 years ago, are prone to look back and comment upon the changes which time hath wrought, both in the personnel of the participants and the manner in which the festival is conducted. . . .

The little company of callers at the ranch home of Col. H. B. Andrews on that Sunday afternoon in the long ago in discussing an attractive entertainment for President Harrison, who was to be the city's guest, April 20, 1891, little dreamed that they were planning a carnival that was to be advertised throughout the land and its value to the city reckoned in dollars and cents.

J. S. Alexander of New York, at that time a San Antonio banker, gave such a delightful description of a flower carnival witnessed in Nice that his ideas were enthusiastically adopted and Mrs. James L. Slayden suggested that it be made a permanent feature of the San Jacinto Day celebration.

Mrs. Slayden called the first meeting, held in the San Antonio Club and presided over by Col. H. B. Andrews, who explained to the large and enthusiastic company what they hoped to do. This seems to have been the first time the club was invaded by women for business purposes, for reporters tell that club members perched in quiet corners consumed with curiosity as to what was to be done next.

At this meeting Mrs. H. D. Kampmann was elected chairman of the ladies' committee, the other members being Mesdames J. H McLeary, C. W. Ogden, W. B. Wright, James L. Slayden, W. W. King, H. B. Andrews, J. J. Stevens, Sam Johnson, Burbank of Fort Sam Houston, A. J. Fry, Edgar Schram, H. P. Drought and John Darragh.

Unfortunately the day President Harrison spent in San Antonio the rain came down in torrents, and a battle was impossible. This did not, however, dampen the ardor of those who had their hearts set on a floral affray, and when a meeting was called a few days later to consider the matter the cry was, "On with the battle!" and thus it happened that the first Flower Battle was fought April 24, 1891.

This first battle was purely a social event, only friends and neighbors and the descendants of the Texas veterans participating, and for that reason there was much enthusiasm and gaiety, and the touch of patriotism that has been missing in the Carnivals after the commercial side predominated.

In this first battle only natural flowers were used, and it was a real floral battle. The marshals were Will Tobin, John Green, Dr. G. G. Watts and Officer Schumacher. The old Belknap Rifles acted as guards, and were the only representatives of military life. The procession formed on Nacogdoches Street, passing down Houston to Navarro, west on Navarro to College, north on College to St. Mary's, west on St. Mary's to Commerce, around Military Plaza, and east on Commerce to Alamo Plaza, where the most spirited battle in the whole history of the Carnival was fought.

Among the attractive turnouts which has lived in the memory of all was that of Mrs. W. W. King. Her beautiful span of yellow Arabian horses [drew] a handsome carriage which was elaborately trimmed with Marechal Nell roses. Yellow ribbons were used for lines. Mrs. Maverick and Mrs. Milton Vance entered a float filled with little Mavericks, Vances, Bells and Frasers. The team of Dr. Herff, Sr. was driven by his son, Charles, and filled with little Herffs. Mrs. Madrasz drove a stylish phaeton trimmed with Easter lilies, and riding with her was Mrs. Will Herff.

Mr. and Mrs. H. B. Andrews were in a beautifully trimmed victoria and Master Barclay Andrews was in a phaeton drawn by four Shetland ponies. He had with him little Miss Schreiver. Mrs. J. Riely Gordon entered a float, and with her were Misses Newton, French, Florian, Hunt, Cerone, Dow, and Hutton. These ladies were all dressed to represent flowers, and greeted with applause all along the line. James Simpson, Robert Green, Wright and Baker were in a dilapidated outfit, a relic of San Jacinto. Among the other well-known people whose carriages appeared were Mrs. B. F. Yoakum, Mrs. C. W. Ogden, the children of J. J. Stevens riding in a beautiful pony cart. Miss Stapp was the only lady bicyclist in the first parade.

Much Spanish moss and ribbon grace, also palm branches, were used in the trimming of the carriages. The ladies all superintended their own decorations, did much of the work themselves and paid all the bills. General Stanley and Major Burbank viewed the battle from the San Antonio Club. Mr. and Mrs. Castleman, who were staying at the Cable ranch, came in to witness the sport and were the targets for many a floral missile.

This first Carnival proved such a success that by the next year the whole town was ready to participate. . . .

In 1892, under the leadership of Mrs. J. J. Stevens, the celebration assumed much larger proportions. In addition to the flower parade there was a trades display, and the fire department formed an important part of the parade. Paper flowers were largely used in the decorations, and enterprising women were already on the grounds to teach us how to make them more beautiful than old Dame Nature herself. The marshals were Robert Green, Alex Walton, James Simpson, George Kues, Jr., B. C. Reily and L. G. Watts.

Very much the same program was carried out in 1893, when Mrs. James French was the president. The veterans were given a prominent place in the procession. They were Capt. McMaster, H. P. Bee, Nat Mitchell and Sam McCullough.

Mrs. John Fraser was president in 1894–95, and did much hard work toward arousing interest, as the novelty had by this time worn off. In 1895 the battle was postponed until June 10, and was a feature of the entertainment during the national convention of the Travelers' Protective Association. In 1896, in order to revive, if possible, the spirit of patriotism which characterized the first battles, Mrs. Elizabeth Ogden, one of the Texas pioneers, was elected president, a position which she held for several years. It was in this year that this festival was first recognized by the War Department, and Secretary Lamont ordered the troops out. Mrs. Ogden and Mrs. Mary Maverick rode in a victoria.

The first San Jacinto Ball was given this year under the auspices of the Daughters of the Republic, and the first queen chosen when

J. CISNEROS

Miss Ida Archer of Austin, a noted Texas beauty, was selected. It precipitated a social war, as many contended that the queen should always be a San Antonio girl. Miss Archer, however, held the position, and Alex Walton was her King. The patronesses were Mesdames J. F. Wade, J. N. Keeran, Ada Waelder, Gilbert Smith, Frank Grice, E. B. Chandler, Albert Joske, J. H. McLeary, R. V. Culberson, Goodman, M. Halff and B. C. Reily. Leon Goodman was the page. Those who danced before royalty were Laura Grice, Zula Nash and Ruth Peebles.

The social feature of 1897 was the grand cotton ball given under the auspices of the Daughters of the Republic. Miss Mae Cresson was queen and Clinton Kearney king. Master Frank Paschal was page. Prizes were offered for the first time for the best display in the various classes.

A touch of sadness as well as a thrill of patriotism was added to the Carnival of 1898, for at noon, on April 21, the whistles blew announcing war with Spain was declared.

In 1899 the day closed with a grand ball given at Beethoven Hall. Miss Emma Reed was the queen and George Gosling, king. Robert Kampmann and Wilbur Moss were pages.

In 1900 Carnival week was noted for the number of conventions meeting in this city. A pleasing feature of the entertainment was the living flag of school children formed on the plaza. The day closed with a grand military ball. Miss Lola Kokernot was the queen and Thomas Conroy, king. Dances and many spectacular features were introduced. Governor and Mrs. Sayers were guests of honor.

Mrs. J. J. Stevens was president again in 1901, and Ben Hammond, chief director. In 1902 the Business Men's Club was in control, and a ball was given at night for the benefit of the free clinic. Beautiful floats were a conspicuous feature of the 1903 Carnival. The day closed with a ball for the benefit of the Alamo purchase fund. Gen. and Mrs. Fred Grant were guests of honor at the social functions.

The Carnival of 1904 was conspicuous for the large number of beautiful turnouts. Miss Clara Driscoll and Judge Clarence Martin were in Mrs. Kampmann's victoria, which was trimmed with American beauty roses. Mrs. S. G. Newton and Mrs. William Aubrey won much praise for their sunflower turnout. For several years Sam Bennett carried off the first prize both on account of his artistic decorations and his beautiful team.

In 1905 King Selamat I made his appearance and was well represented by D. J. Woodward. Miss Clara Driscoll was crowned queen on Alamo Plaza just in front of the Alamo, for which she had worked so zealously. Frank Bushick was general director in 1906. There were many street attractions and a battle of confetti every night. A baby show was also a prominent feature. King Selamat II was represented by Arthur Guenther. . . . The Selamat dynasty closed in 1907 with Selamat III represented by J. H. Kirkpatrick. Miss Leonora Hummel was the queen and Will Tobin chairman of the Flower Battle committee

In 1908 The Flower Battle Association was organized with Mrs S. G. Newton as president, a position which she has held ever since. This association is composed of the most prominent ladies in the city, and is entirely separate from the Carnival Association. The queen is now chosen by the Order of the Alamo, an organization of young men who have charge of the Queen's Ball. The duchesses are selected from all the neighboring towns, and these, with the princesses and knights, form the queen's court.

In 1908 the queen for the first time was chosen from the Army. Miss Bertha Rowalle filled this exalted position and Gen. Jesse M. Lee was the prime minister. In 1909 Miss Eda Kampmann was the Queen and Miss Julia Armstrong her lady in waiting and Joe Frost prime minister. The court scene was a very brilliant one. Miss Nana Davenport was the Queen in 1910 with Claude Coleman her lady in waiting and Wallace Newton prime minister.

— Marin B. Fenwick, *San Antonio Express*, March 26, 1911

14.
Leap Year Plans

They had already determined with rare, feminine unanimity that it was incumbent on them as up-to-date women that they should give a leap year party, so when they met the other morning all they had to do was decide on the details.

To older and wiser heads these details would have appeared formidable indeed, but the dash and spirit with which the dear girls began the consideration of these details evinced but a light appreciation of the task. There were probably two dozen of them there, and, being San Antonio girls, of course were all pretty, and with the superinduced vivacity that comes from enthusiasm.

The early arrivals passed their time waiting for their belated sisters in discussing leap year in the abstract. Discussion as to the propriety of availing themselves of the traditional rights was becoming so animated that the fair young hostess—a demure little girl, disposed to agree with everyone—brought the discussion to an abrupt end by announcing that the business of the meeting should be taken up immediately. Then they formed a circle around the center table to "consider the details."

There was rather an embarrassing silence for a moment until a young girl who lives out on San Pedro Avenue gulped down a half masticated caramel and inquired how many would be invited. Immediately twenty-four young heads were thrown into a "brown study," for it was evident this detail hadn't even been thought of, and its introduction was unexpected. A period of absolute silence followed save for the throbbing of twenty-four young brains. The throbbing increased with each moment, and the ticking of the hall-clock—a big thirty-day affair—was hushed. The house began to sway, and several plates fell from the breakfast table. The throbbing continued and was beginning to [move] the gate posts outside when a young girl who lives up on Laurel Heights jumped up and steadying herself by clutching the swinging center table, exclaimed, "I've got it!"

The house stopped swaying and the chickens in the back yard emerged cautiously from their coops, as twenty-three young brains stopped throbbing to inquire, "Oh, what is it?"

"Everybody we know!" screamed the Laurel Heights maiden, and then twenty-four plump young ladies dropped back in their chairs exhausted, while the chickens outside began to cackle with something of their accustomed vigor and the cat came back from the yard, whither it had fled when the house began to rock. In about five minutes there were signs of returning animation in the group of pretty femininity.

"How ever did you think of that?" inquired a dark-eyed girl languidly, as she straightened up and passed her hand across her brow as if to assure herself that she really existed. "Oh yes, do tell us, like a dear!" pleaded a tall, stately looking young girl whose coiffure had become disarranged during the excitement.

The Laurel Heights maiden lay back as if in a faint, and not until she had partaken of a cup of tea that had been hastily brought did she show signs of revivication. "Well, now, come up close," she whispered, "and I'll tell you."

They all crowded around, and while three of the dears fanned her the Laurel Heights maiden traced her syllogism to its conclusion. "You see," she began faintly, "we couldn't invite just twenty-four men, or one beau for each girl, for you know some of us have two and three."

"Of course!" assented a young King William Street maiden with blond hair. "No, never, for how ever could I invite Jake and not invite Tom?" exclaimed a young girl whose home is one of the prettiest houses on Avenue C.

"Well," the Laurel Heights maiden continued, after taking another sip of tea and, having a pillow arranged under her head, "of course we couldn't fix any definite number to every girl, so then I thought everybody we knew!" and she fell back exhausted.

"How wonderful!" exclaimed a young girl paying rapt attention from an ottoman on the floor. "Isn't it just lovely!" exclaimed another. "You poor dear thing. I just knew you were brilliant!" purred a sympathetic little dark-haired maiden as she reached over and kissed the Laurel Heights maiden on the cheek. "Really, Kit"—her name's Kate—"you can just think dreadfully deep!" assured another. Then they all resumed their places and the secretary, who was agreed on unanimously, recorded in a little tablet . . . "First, invite everybody we know."

"Well now, girls," spoke up the dear who had led the thought, "we must next decide what kind of refreshments we shall have."

"Oh, dear, won't we never get through," complained a young girl who didn't like going back into the throes of thought. "Now come on, girls," the chairwoman remonstrated persuasively, "let's get at it and show the men how easily we can do these things. They just make such a fuss and flurry every time they get up a little entertainment, that, really, you'd think the management of all the planets were confided to them. Now, there's a dear; let's go on and do the thing right. . . ."

"Well," and she nagged at her handkerchief as if not certain that her idea would be well received, "I think turkey sandwich would be nice." There was, however, a unanimous concurrence of opinion; and the secretary recorded in her list of details: "Second—Turkey sandwich." Then the chairwoman urged all the young heads to resume their thinking, the Laurel Heights maiden, however, being excused.

The next report was quick in forthcoming. Indeed, not a vibration was felt when the presence of another idea was proclaimed. The possessor of it immediately unloaded it by saying, "chicken salad!" This idea wasn't very well received. One dear said it came too easy. As a matter of fact its coming didn't produce a single vibration of the house. It was quite evident that this idea wasn't considered a very profound one. One girl exclaimed: "The inevitable chicken salad, indeed!" Another said it would make the affair too much of a masculine kind.

A spirited debate followed as to the admissibility of chicken salad. It seemed certain that chicken salad would be cast out, when the parent of the idea diplomatically compromised by suggesting that it be accepted subject to reconsideration. This was agreed to, and the secretary recorded: "Third—Chicken salad. (Subject to reconsideration)."

Then twenty-four young minds again relapsed into thought. It was soon evident that a gigantic idea was in process of evolution, for again the house began to rock. The chandelier began to tinkle. The piano began to sway. A statue fell right at the feet of the chairwoman, and there was a crash of china in the dining room. The cat was seen to fly through the hall (figuratively speaking) and fierce howls which floated in from the yard indicated that the cat had collided with the fleeing dog.

The chickens ran about as if a hawk was circling over them, a vase of flowers sitting in the southeast corner of the room toppled over. Twenty-four young ladies were clutching grimly to twenty-four chairs which were oscillating like the pendulum of grandfather's clock. Twenty-four pairs of pretty teeth were set desperately, and there was grim determination depicted on twenty-four pretty, but pallid faces. The house was beginning to oscillate with the long, steady swing of a grapevine swing when one of the dears gasped faintly: "I've got one!"

The house stopped rocking, the cat came back, the dog returned to his sunny couch on the porch and tranquility again reigned.

Twenty-three pairs of haggard eyes looked beseechingly toward the chair whence the sound came. But there was no response. The figure toward which they looked so appealingly was apparently lifeless. The head hung forward on the breast, the arms dropped limp. The dears immediately crowded about, a little tea and a glass of water were brought and soon there were signs of returning life. Presently there was a deep, pathetic sigh and then two weary, pretty eyes opened, and two luscious cherry lips parted, and there came faintly from between them the word "celery!" while the dear fainted away again. Everybody said, "Oh, of course!" and the secretary wrote: "Fourth—Celery."

It was unanimously agreed this dear should be excused, but as the Laurel Heights girl recovered there were still twenty-four young minds to evolve ideas for the leap year party. However, it was very

evident that the task was becoming irksome, for the chairwoman had to urge them vigorously before they would relapse into thought.

But the minds were becoming prolific under practice. Scarcely had they become settled than the birth of two ideas was proclaimed almost simultaneously. One was "turkeys," the other "chickens." Everybody admitted the profundity of these ideas. Even the dear who had evolved the idea of celery roused herself enough to express her concurrence. So the secretary wrote: "Fifth—Turkeys. Sixth—Chickens." There was a beam of satisfaction whose radiance lighted the room directly above, as the dears noted the growing length of the secretary's memorandum.

However, it was short-lived, for immediately someone inquired: "But how many turkeys?" The query had a startling effect, and a pained expression came where but a moment before there was only radiance. "Of course," observed one demure little girl, who had not contributed to the stock of ideas, and who, in fact, had been very subdued, "one will not be enough."

"Oh, dear no, of course not," chimed in she who had produced the idea. Some degree of relief was manifested at this progress in determining that one turkey would not be sufficient. One girl suggested that five would be about the required number. "Now, let's go at this matter logically," pleaded a rather plump young girl, who parts her hair in the middle and wears glasses. "How many people will be there? About 100, don't you think?" Everybody did, and the complacency increased as the tangle began to be unraveled. "Well, then," the girl with the glasses resumed, "we ought to have about fifty turkeys."

The consensus of opinion was that this number was too high. One young girl, who prefaced her remarks by saying that she had attended a cooking school, said thirty would certainly suffice. But just as many thought this number too low as who thought 50 would be too high, and it began to look as if there would be a deadlock, when the young dear who had given the celery idea said meekly: "Why not make it forty?"

"Oh, you sweet little dear," several exclaimed as they rushed over to kiss her. "Your little head is just awfully full of sense!" observed one, who, after waiting for the others to give osculatory evidence of their gratitude, had kissed her on the forehead with more deliberation. Both sides accepted the compromise and the secretary wrote behind the fifth item: (40). It was decided with much dispatch comparatively that twenty chickens would be sufficient, and the secretary added "20" to the sixth item.

"And then we must have some cakes," suddenly exclaimed one of the dears with the force of one endowed with an inspiration. "Oh, dear, yes," everyone assented. The question of the number again came up perplexingly, but it was decided that 20—if they were big ones—would be sufficient. Then the secretary wrote: "Twenty cakes. (Big ones)."

"And, oh, yes, we must have some wine!" declared a vivacious dear whose hair is golden. The correctness of this was unanimously assented, though there was some diversion of opinion as to the quantity. It was compromised, however, like the turkey item and the secretary wrote: "Eighth—Wine—Forty gallons."

The chairwoman again urged the dears to relax into thought, but there was open rebellion. Most declared the menu was complete, "for," she explained, "you know it's not going to be a banquet, but just a light refreshment—a lunch." The chairwoman didn't persist, but admonished them that there were other details to decide on. "When shall we hold the party?" she asked. "And will we walk the men there or shall we ride them? If we ride shall it be in buses, trolley cars or in carriages?" The opinion was unanimous that they ought to be conveyed to the party in carriages, "Cause, you know," explained one of them, "if we set the precedent of trolley cars or busses won't they adopt it next year?"

One of the dears said she knew she'd be married before next year, so that that argument didn't appeal to her, but that she would favor carriages for the sake of others. Indignant glances athwart the room, but open hostilities were avoided by a consideration of the cost of carriages. One girl expressed the opinion that all the carriages necessary to convey the 100 would not cost more than $10.

Everybody declared this estimate was extravagant. Some thought a $3 appropriation would be sufficient for this item, but on the advice of others $5 were set aside for this purpose. As a further assurance, however, one dear suggested that the party be held in Turner Hall, whose location was so central, she remarked, that the carriage hire could not exceed $5. So the secretary wrote: "Ninth—Carriages, $5."

The dears then looked around as if for something more to grapple with and dispose of. The chairwoman, as if divining the meaning remarked: "Well, we're through. See how quickly and completely we have decided on our plans and made our arrangements. Could the men do it in double the time or half so completely?" There was a general shaking of heads, until the dear with the celery idea said: "How about the money? What is it going to cost?"

The sudden appearance of a leper in an orphanage wouldn't have created more consternation. An "Oh!" swept through the room and wafted the dog off the front porch. The chairwoman fainted, and tears rushed to the eyes of everyone. When the chairwoman recovered she suggested an adjournment, and, naming Monday as the time for the next meeting, the dears pulled their veils down tightly over their faces, and giving their adieus in whispers, silently went away.

— *San Antonio Express*, January 25, 1896

15.
The Library Women

"Smoke one less cigar a day and contribute the money saved to a public library" is the slogan originated by a group of Fort Worth club women in the closing years of the nineteenth century, which began the series of Carnegie Libraries all over the United States. . . .

While less spontaneous, the origin of the San Antonio Carnegie Library, which was the second one given by the steel magnate, was equally picturesque and equally the result of the untiring and ingenious efforts of public spirited women, although it did not come as the immediate result of one successful campaign but of years of patient struggle and determined effort. Credit for the actual Carnegie gift of $50,000 for a public library in San Antonio has been generally given to Mrs. James L. Slayden, whose husband, James L. Slayden was for many years Congressman of this district, and associated with Carnegie both personally and on committees. . . .

The Carnegie Library was the distinct outgrowth of two libraries, which in turn had a predecessor in a still earlier library which was formed by private contributions of books, shortly after the Civil War, and flourished throughout the '70s. The organization was known as the Alamo Literary Society, and kept several thousand books which had been accumulated in a large one-room stone building on Houston Street on property belonging to the Maverick estate, about where the Jefferson Hotel is now located. The "Library," as it was proudly called, was a popular meeting place where debuts were held and concerts given, but its reading facilities were entirely inadequate to the size of the city even then and means of providing a suitable library for San Antonio as a necessity of civic growth was constantly discussed.

Finally, Sam Maverick offered to donate the site then used to the city, if a suitable library building was erected and plans for such a structure were accepted on October 30, 1872. The stone building was begun, partially completed and even used for a time, but no funds were available and after a time it fell into disuse, the books were scattered, and active work as a public library for San Antonio was abandoned as a dream hopeless of accomplishment.

About 1890, however, a library movement was begun again in good earnest by a group of younger women of St. Mary's Church, led by Miss Marie Sheldon. They organized the Alamo Free Library with personal contributions of books which were kept by Miss Sheldon in the belfry room of old St. Mary's Church on St. Mary's Street. The Alamo Library proved so popular and people showed themselves so book-hungry that larger quarters were soon required, and a tiny frame building on Commerce Street, next to the Messenger Printing Office, was rented. Prominent in this organization was Mrs. Henry Drought, who was a member of the first board of directors and its president almost from the time of organization until it was merged with the other San Antonio Library into the present Carnegie Library.

A lively account is given by Mrs. Drought of the workings of "this first poor little library," as she calls it, in which frequent bazaars and balls given to raise funds for the library maintenance form the leading features.

We really began the Alamo Library with $10. Mrs. Corbett, who lived on South Flores Street, gave the first $5, and Mr. Drought gave the second $5 and we just trusted to luck to get the rest of the money when we had to have it. By the time we had grown some more with $14.00 made at one bazaar and $9.25 made at another one—and the different women interested in the library did work so hard for every cent we got to run it with—we had got about 1,000 books together, and felt well enough established to move into better quarters.

We rented that long one-story stone building that ran down the north end of the old Twohig yard on St. Mary's Street, which had been left to Bishop Neary or Bishop Forrest, I have forgotten which, and moved into that. We had to pay $75 a year for the rooms, and it seemed like a million dollars to us. We had made the library entirely free when we moved into the Twohig yard, and with all that rent and salary we paid Miss Healey, our librarian, poor as it was, we just had to have one ball right after another, with bazaars in between, to keep it going at all. Still, with all the work we did and the endless anxiety about getting money to carry on with, we were very proud indeed that the Alamo Library was the second free library in Texas, the Rosenberg Library in Galveston antedating ours . . . by a short time.

Associated with Mrs. Drought as directors of the library were Mrs. William Cassin, Mrs. T. M. Conroy, and Mrs. B. F. Kingsley. Somewhat later, about 1893, the San Antonio Public Library was organized, with a woman's exchange and day nursery as important features, with Mrs. H. D. Kampmann as prime mover and Mrs. Dan Ainsworth, Mrs. Charles Wilson (now Mrs. J. F. B. Beckwith), Mrs. Eli Hertzberg, Mrs. John J. Stevens, Mrs. Burbank, whose husband was stationed at Fort Sam Houston, and about a dozen other women deeply interested and concerned in its development.

According to Mrs. Beckwith, who served as secretary of the San Antonio Public Library almost from its organization until it was merged with the Alamo Library into the Carnegie, the first quarters of this organization were also on Maverick property in one room rented from Albert Maverick in a building on the corner where the Gibbs Building now stands.

In those days the library circle was a group of the socially elect. You didn't offer to join until you had been invited, and if you didn't belong to the library you were a rank outsider. For all it was so socially important—or maybe because of it, you never can tell—the library had an awful struggle for existence and the usual feminine resources of balls, parties and bazaars were exploited from every angle to raise funds to carry on with.

Every year a Library Benefit Ball was given in Beethoven Hall that was the leading social function of the spring season, and according to old gossip of the closing years of the Nineteenth Century, the present San Jacinto Cotillion Club was the outgrowth of a red-hot discussion as to whether the ball given as the main social function of Fiesta Week of 1893 or '95—I have forgotten which—with the queen and her attendants present, should be an invitation ball or the regular library benefit.

Mrs. Kampmann, who was a good deal like John Gilpin's wife in the old poem "For though on pleasure she was bent, she had a frugal mind," insisted that the Fiesta Ball could be just as distinguished socially if it were turning an honest penny for the library at the same time. The San Antonio Cotillion Club was the result of the discussion, and there were two balls that year instead of one.

All our efforts to make money for the library reached a climax, in 1897, however, with a "Kermesse" in which everybody in town took part. It was given for three nights in the old Grand Opera House to crowded audiences. The library board had out between six and seven hundred dollars as the highest goal they could hope to reach but when returned and counted, we found we had close to $1,400. We couldn't believe it at first and were almost wild with pride and satisfaction.

With the money made on the "Kermesse" the old John Herff house on Losoya Street, about where the Losoya Hotel now stands, was rented and the library with about 1,000 books moved into the front downstairs room, the woman's exchange into the next room and the day nursery into the back room and the back yard. About two years later the nursery was dropped and a little later the exchange died a natural death, but the library continued to grow and flourish with the money we had made, the book fines and the $2 a year dues that were charged, and such frequent parties were no longer necessary. During this time Miss Fannie Kerr, now Mrs. J. W. Fuller, was librarian. . . .

The definite offer of a library for San Antonio contained in the letter from Carnegie's secretary to Mrs. Slayden was presented to Marshall Hicks as mayor, in the form of a letter from Judge A. W. Houston by a committee of women from both libraries, headed by Mrs. Mary Howard as chairman. With the formal acceptance of the generous offer by the mayor and city council, on February 5, 1900, $50 a month was allowed from the city for the upkeep of each library until the new building could be completed.

After much discussion as to a suitable location, the site of the present library was offered to the city by Mrs. Caroline Kampmann, with the proviso that the property would immediately revert to heirs of the Kampmann estate if it were ever used for any purpose other than a library site. It was accepted after some controversy and delay, plans were asked for the building, bids made and work begun. However, it was nearly two years after the original Carnegie gift was made before the library was completed and available for public use, in June, 1903.

Books from the two libraries which were turned over to the city as the nucleus of the original library stock numbered something over 7,500 volumes and gifts from each included many souvenirs and collections of value and interest.

— Penelope Bordon, *San Antonio Express*, June 5, 1927

16.
Mrs. Beretta's Bluebonnets

Will Texas refuse to wear her bluebonnet this spring and thus disappoint the artists who have been waiting patiently to catch a glimpse of her colorful raiment, and the tourists who came to Texas just to see her in bluebonnet time and all her adoring homefolks as well? . . .

It was Mrs. J. K. Beretta of San Antonio who first sent out the warning call and started the now statewide movement to save them.

Mrs. Beretta was, at the time, president of the City Federation of Women's Clubs of San Antonio. During the hot months while many women were at the seashore or the mountains she worked unceasingly at her plans. She gathered information from all sections of the state relative to the rapid disappearance of the flower. She gathered all the lyrical, legendary and historical literature about the bluebonnet possible to procure. This she studied and, selecting the most vivid in appeal, she arranged with trained speakers, singers and readers to present it.

She did more. With a few friends whose interest in the work she enlisted she went into the fields and open spaces about San Antonio and gathered bluebonnet seed. Breaking off the portions of the plants that held the seed, the gatherers would toss them into open, inverted parasols and in this way brought them back to town with small loss. Later they opened the pods and sorted the tiny seed.

In this manner they gathered several pounds, and, remembering that each bluebonnet plant bears only a very small fraction of an ounce of seed, one realizes what a big task they accomplished. Mrs. Beretta had also arranged with some Austin agencies to save seeds for her to insure an abundance for her purpose.

The opening Federation luncheon of 1922–23 will long be remembered in San Antonio. Her plans by now being widely known, attendance was unprecedented. The room chosen for the luncheon overflowed so that tables had to be placed in the halls. The decorations were great refreshing bowls of splendidly healthy looking bluebonnets.

"Why," exclaimed every woman upon entering, almost as if it were part of the program, "where in the world did you get bluebonnets in October?" At which the previously initiated would laugh.

"These," explained Mrs. Beretta, "are, as you can see if you look closely, all made of tissue paper. I am glad you like them for I assure you it is the only kind of bluebonnet Texas will know anything about in a few years if we do not take heed to the destruction that is going on in our fields."

Then, in that earnest way that has made her so popular throughout the State, and with her eyes alight with a crusader's enthusiasm, she launched her appeal to save the little state flower from utter annihilation. Her program in its entirety was a splendid appeal for the bluebonnets.

A botanical expert whom she introduced added the weight of his masculine approval to this distinctly feminine move. He went into the history and the nature of the lupine, told in impressive technical terms of its value to the soil and explained how its salvation could be accomplished.

"It is an unselfish little plant," he said. "It grows in poor soil scorned by other beauties of the field. It enriches the soil speedily as do all legumes and then moves on to poorer places to continue its service. It is hardy and kind and beautiful, being one of our few really blue flowers."

The singers sang of the bluebonnets and the readers and speakers did their part. Then the carefully hoarded seed was distributed, each club delegate and guest receiving a tiny package with explicit instructions how to plant them.

"Scatter them over your yard in the fall," Mrs. Beretta told them. "Do not mow your yard in the spring until they have come up, bloomed and gone to seed which they do very early. After that you may mow as much as you like and feel assured of a lovely blue carpet of them the following spring."

And one seeing Mrs. Beretta's own yard in the springs of 1923 and 1924 could entertain no doubt as to the efficacy of her method.

The delegates carried her message and her enthusiasm to their respective clubs. The endorsement was unanimous. Indeed, it seemed that all Texas nature lovers had been but waiting for her to speak.

— Evantha Caldwell, *San Antonio Express*, April 19, 1925

Part III
Legendary Stories

Fact and fiction have long been part of the San Antonio legacy. No settings have been more favored than the Alamo and the other missions as the backdrops for these myths and legends with their romances, ghosts, and the inevitable underground tunnels between mission and mission or mission and river.

Richard Wallace Buckley grew up just north of the Alamo grounds in the Irish Flat. Son of a popular policeman, the author of "A Tale of the Alamo" enjoyed a local reputation as a fiction writer. He published at least one full-length novel.

Charles Merritt Barnes deserved his reputation as San Antonio's best-known feature writer as a regular contributor to the *Express*. He based his book *Combats and Conquests of Immortal Heroes* (1910) on his newspaper articles, but unfortunately the published volume is not as well written, nor are the stories so complete, as in their original form.

A knowledgeable octogenerian, who in his youth knew Barnes, has suggested that the stories in the *Express* had the advantage of the services of an editor, while the published volume did not. Certainly the report of the funeral pyres along the Alameda and memoirs of the Garza homestead, as well as earlier stories in this volume, are not so meaningful in *Combats and Conquests*. San Antonio's most indefatigable interviewer of early settlers who survived at the turn of the century deserves recognition for his appreciation of oral history long before the tape recorder popularized this memoir form.

Richard Wallace Buckley also was author of the legend of Mission Concepción. The reader will recognize certain similarities between it and the tale of the Alamo. Both involve an element of mystery, a similarity of prose, a surprise ending and the obvious O. Henry influence. The author of the legend of Mission Espada remains ànonymous.

Elements of truth are incorporated in the strange tale of the bride and the turkey at Mission Espada. Father Bouchou, long the revered priest at Espada, and Justice Chavagneux were certainly not fictional characters, and a number of families still lived along the walls of this mission. More fact than fiction appears in this story, which is not commonly known in local legend.

17.
A Tale of the Alamo

After many stealthy and sinuous windings through the "vast howling wilderness" of Western Texas, the Mexican army of invasion, 4,000 strong, lay encamped on the Leon, seven miles from San Antonio. As Lieutenant Cordoña, in the garb of a ranchero, galloped rapidly ahead on that dreary afternoon of February 23, 1836, his thoughts grew busy with a subject utterly foreign to the scouting service, which, at his own request, had been assigned him by General Santa Anna.

He was in the thrall of a fascinating image that had haunted him like a vision of Paradise since he left these parts three months before. He knew that he did wrong to entertain this vision. He felt that he had no right to indulge the wild, tormenting dream of winning the hand of the fair-haired daughter of an alien race, against which his country was now waging a merciless war. He felt, keenly felt, the incongruity of his conduct, as, in counterfeit guise, he thus sped onward to seek an interview with the object of his infatuation.

Yet what ardent swain is there who may philosophize with love, or be daunted by the minor scruples of conscience? Certainly not Santos Cordoña, in whose veins flowed the hot blood of Castile and Mexico. Rapturously, therefore, he rode on, abandoning himself to the memory of his romantic meeting with Ruth Burgess in the preceding autumn.

It was dawn on the morning of October 28, just after the first, short battle of the Texas revolution, which took place on the river near the old Mission Concepción, two miles south of San Antonio. He had been shot in the thigh, and while he lay there with 65 of his dead comrades and nearly twice as many wounded, listening to the yells of the victorious Texans and straining his aching eyes to see the lurid eastern skyline, whither pursued and pursuers had vanished, she came.

Emerging from a low-browed adobe farmhouse not far off, a slender girlish figure, carrying a bucket of water, bravely advanced to the scene of the recent conflict and stole softly, hither and thither, under the shadows of the huge pecan trees, ministering to the wounded. Bless her! Already his fevered brain clothed this angel of the "foughten field" with a holy glamor. Before she reached him, however, he swooned, overcome by loss of blood and fatigue.

When he recovered consciousness he found himself in a neat little room in the home of Nathan Burgess, the father of the girl whose mission of mercy had attracted his fading vision on the field of battle. Returning with the rest of the Texans from the pursuit of the fleeing Mexicans, Burgess, seeing that the crippled man was an officer, and moved with compassion for him, had obtained permission from General Burleson, the patriot commander, to have him conveyed to his own home, where he could secure more careful treatment than might be accorded his wounded comrades.

Thus it was that Santos Cordoña came under the roof of one of his recent enemies, who, by a turn of the wheel of fate, had now become his friend. There, in the home of the young lady whose beauty, bravery and devotion had infatuated him, he spent three weeks of convalescence, nursed alternately by her and an old serving woman of his own race, named Niña.

Ah, those brief, far too brief, days of convalescence! As he now recalled them after the lapse of three months, he sighed heavily, and urged his staunch little Spanish horse to increase speed. How happy he had been while in her presence, breathing the same air, and noting the tender solicitude for his recovery in her low, soft voice, in her sweet, expressive blue eyes!

Those only who have loved know the potency of such approximation, and he had grown to love his fair, little Anglo-Saxon "rebel" with all the mad, wild passion of his people. Aye, and he had prepared himself to tell her so on the evening when, through the clemency of his captors, he was about to depart for his father's ranch on the Nueces, if---

A disquieting reflection broke in upon his reveries. He fell sullen for a moment and a sinister shadow forced its way over his strong, dark face. On that last memorable evening with her, their converse had been interrupted by the arrival of a tall, bronzed, square-shouldered American, in whose presence the eyes of his beloved brightened, her pink cheeks went red. "Who was he? What was he to her?" he asked himself now as he had asked himself then. Could this strange man have been other than a friend? But---

Away with suspicion! Loyal to the sanguine hopes of his devoted heart, he straightened himself in the saddle, brushed the uneasy phantom of jealousy aside, and rode on with recovered composure. He shaped his course to the south of the town, along the banks of the beautiful river which here, jutting in and out, trills its ceaseless melody to the ancient mission church of Concepción.

Turning into a copse by the roadside, he soon drew up before the trellised porch of the well-remembered little cottage. Ruth Burgess was surprised, though so evidently pleased to see him again that he straightway mistook the significance of her cordial welcome. Doubt took wings and flew; hope sprang mountain high. He observed, however, as he seated himself opposite her on the porch, that the pink blossom had gone from her cheeks and that she wore a plain, muslin mourning gown. Still he thought that she looked more pretty than ever, with her wonderful white skin made luminous by the uncombed hair flowing over her shoulders in golden waves.

"Why, Señor Cordoña! What a pleasant surprise! Indeed, you are the last person in the world I expected to see in San Antonio at this time. I thought you intended staying on your father's ranch till the war was over!"

"I am here on business, señorita," he returned, evasively. A few desultory commonplaces followed, when he asked with much concern:

"Why does the señorita look sad and wear mourning?"

"Alas, señor, I have good reason to be sad! My poor father is no more. He took pneumonia from exposure during the winter campaign and died a week before Christmas, leaving me and my little brother orphaned, alone and well-nigh unprotected in these perilous times. There is nobody but old Juan, the husband of Niña,

to keep up the farm. Sometimes I feel so bereft and lonely that I almost wish I were dead."

With Latin-Aztec impetuosity he seized the opportunity her melancholy words afforded.

"Dear Ruth," he pleaded passionately, "permit me the sweet privilege of being your friend and protector, for only God knows, brave little girl, how much I love you."

She made a shrinking gesture, but, unheeding, he hurried on:

"Ah, señorita, can you be surprised that I love you. I, a wild product of the prairies, with little or no ties of affection until I saw you? Your image, first impressed on my mind in so unusual and romantic a manner, has become everything to me. I have cherished it, loved it, as only a man of my nature can. It is true you met me as a soldier fighting the cause in which your father was engaged; still, I know that your sense of honor does not blame me for being loyal to my country; true, my people yet war with yours, but that is a weak obstacle to love.

"I come of good race, was educated in one of the schools of your country, and speak your language almost as well as my own! I have ample means at present and my father's promise that I will one day inherit his large hacienda. Oh, Ruth, bid me hope that when this miserable war is over---"

"Stop, señor!" she interrupted at last, "your avowal of love grieves me very much. I am extremely sorry; oh, so very sorry, señor! I know you to be a brave, generous man, whose heart any woman, even I, might have been proud to win, only----"

She paused, blushed and resumed with modestly averted eyes: "Before I knew you, señor, I was bethrothed to another. I have promised to marry him immediately after the war, should he survive it."

Cordoña winced under the unlooked-for blow, his head dropped, his lips parted, and again the sinister shadow moved over his dusky face.

"Is it the big, brawny frontiersman who came when I last spoke with you here?" he queried, ungraciously.

"Yes," she replied simply. "Ross Kemble."

"How long have you known him?"

"Ever since we came here from Tennessee, three years ago. He was the best friend father had in Texas."

"There can be no mistake then, you have quite decided to marry him?"

"Yes, señor, I have."

"Do you love him?"

"Can you ask, señor? I have said that I intend to marry him."

"Ah! true, forgive me. Where is he now?"

"In the fortress of the Alamo, with Travis, Crockett, Bowie and the other Texans."

The man clutched the crown of the large sombrero he held in his lap, convulsively. His lustrous black eyes grew big with a momentary look of triumph. Then he put down the mood when, glancing at his companion again, he saw that she was weeping—weeping, poor little creature, as though she had purposely done him some grievous injury. Remorseful pity for her drove every other feeling from his breast. Reaching under the folds of his cloak, he produced a crumpled sheet of paper.

"Do not weep, little friend; it is not your fault. Try to forget my rash declaration of love. There is another motive for my visit which concerns you more than my misplaced affection. It is this." He handed her the paper. "That is a certificate of favor and amity to the inmates of the house, signed by General Santa Anna."

"Santa Anna," she echoed, breathlessly, "do not, oh, do not tell me, señor, that he is near San Antonio!"

Again he took refuge in evasion: "Do not alarm yourself unnecessarily. Thinking of you, as I have done, unfortunately, every waking minute since I left here, I secured this paper a month ago, while the army was at Guerrero, although I had very little idea then, nor have I now, that any of your people will be molested in their private capacities. However, it is well to take every precaution for safety in such unbridled times as these. It is expected, of course, that the army will move in this direction soon, but you have nothing to dread. You have had trouble enough, señorita, pray do not distress yourself with imaginary fears."

There was an awkward pause. He could not trust himself to further prolong the interview, and, rising, walked to his horse, she walking by his side. After swinging himself into the saddle, he seemed about to say something more, but reconsidering, merely took the hand she offered him in farewell, and, murmuring "Good-by, God bless you!" was gone, without waiting for a parting word from her.

It was growing late. He knew that the Mexican army was to be upon San Antonio at dark and that he had been commanded to re-join it before it left the Leon, yet he rode slowly along by the side of the river, whose blue-green water showed weirdly black under the twilight shadows.

His mind, meanwhile, was the scene of a singular combat. He was conscious during those high-pitched moments that he had reached the supreme psychic crisis of his young life; that he was sounding depths in his nature hitherto unrevealed. So searching, indeed, was the spirit of introspection that he fancied he could even trace the filmy line of demarcation between the Aztec and Spanish strains so curiously blended in his being—between the truculent jealousy of the one and the enobling chivalry of the other.

But above all, he was conscious that the two master passions of his heart—patriotism and love, even hopeless love—were waging a deadly duel in his soul. He realized now, also, that both antagonists in this duel were tyrants in their different ways; country, as typified by the insistent, showy personality of Antonio López de Santa Anna; love, by sweet, womanly, defenseless Ruth Burgess.

Psychologists might well tell us if they do not, that one passion when brought into conflict with another often serves to interpret its fellow with startling distinctness. It seemed so with Cordoña, for, presently, the hard immovable lines of iron resolve straightened out the ruffled, wavering lineaments of the man's gloomy visage.

On whatever side victory lay, whatever moral change had been wrought within him, whatever the result of his reflections, the end came with surprising suddenness. He checked his horse as abruptly as though he were on the brink of a precipice, lifted the broad-brimmed sombrero from his long, flowing black hair, raised his eyes to heaven and exclaimed as one inspired:

"I thank thee, O my God, for this new light! I thank thee that thou hast made the path of my duty plain at last!"

Whirling about, he dashed rapidly back to the home of Ruth Burgess. She saw him coming and went to the gate to meet him. Leaning from his saddle he addressed her in a strangely calm voice:

"Pardon me for returning, señorita; I forgot something I should have said to you. If your lover calls this evening do not, as you value your happiness and his, permit him to go back to the Alamo tonight! I have good reason for the warning. Vow to me that you will do this."

"Oh, señor, your words frighten me very much!" she cried in vague alarm. "What danger threatens him tonight? He has no enemy that I know of and—surely you should bear him no ill-will because of what I told you. Oh, señor, I am so distracted that I hardly know what to think! But surely you could not have the heart to meditate harm to the only protector of a lone and friendless girl!"

"You misunderstood me, Ruth. There is no danger from me. Disabuse your mind of a suspicion that is unworthy of you. It is true that I suffer an irreparable loss—that I go from you a broken-hearted man; still I am no traitor, at least---" he coughed irritably, but without other evidence of confusion, caught up his last two words and went on, "at least believe that I could not be brought to injure anyone who is dear to you. Trust me and say you believe this before I go."

He raised his hat with deferential consideration as he spoke, looking full in her face. The girl cast an anxious, scrutinizing glance up at the intense dark eyes, the serene mouth, the lofty brow, and felt that he was sincere. Taking advantage of her look of confidence, he urged gently:

"If I think it advisable to hold anything in reserve, do not puzzle over it, but promise me solemnly that, should he come you will entreat him not to go back to the Alamo tonight."

"I do promise, señor, and I thank you, although I do not see the necessity for your caution; neither do I expect him tonight, yet I will do as you say, if by chance he comes."

"Good. Did I understand you to say that the old servant, Niña, lives here still, señorita?" he asked with odd irrelevancy.

"Niña? Yes, she is in the kitchen now. Would you like me to call her?"

"No, no, do not disturb her. Give her my best wishes. I am glad to know that the kind old servant remains to help and comfort you in this lonesome place."

He bent a last, lingering look of tenderness upon her.

"I must be off," he said at length, "not to return this time. If we never meet again, señorita, remember always that I was your friend. All I ask in parting is that, in days to come, when you are a happy wife you will sometimes call up a tender thought of one who would willingly die to serve you—to hold your esteem."

The spirit of unconscious resignation, of mournful pathos, with which he said this started the tears to her eyes again. She gave him her hand, which he raised to his lips, and, whispering hoarsely: "God bless and defend you!" left her standing by the gate.

Dusk was coming on. The chill, melancholy wind whistled about the old mission as he clattered past. Rounding a turn to the left, he shot like an arrow through the dry mesquite thicket and in ten minutes mounted a rise five miles to the west of the town, where he halted. Jumping to the ground, he fell to pacing to and fro, with the preoccupied air of one who is waiting. It was very quiet, and soon very dark. The muffled night noises of the prairie alone broke the stillness about him. Half an hour elapsed; still his vigilance remained unrewarded.

"I know the army would not delay on my account," he muttered. "Could they have passed before I came? God, if it is too late!"

The thought maddened him. He was about to mount and ride farther on when—hark!—a sound! Throwing himself on the crunched and crackling leaves at his feet, he listened with his ear to the ground. Soon the deep, rhythmic rumble of a multitude of horses' hoofs advancing up the road became distinctly audible. He was in the saddle again and away toward the dim lights of the town, spurring his already much tired horse to a furious burst of speed. He must beat the Mexican army into San Antonio by at least a quarter of an hour! To reach his destination earlier might be injudicious, he reasoned; to delay now would prove fatal to his plan.

The short rest had completely revived the brave, wiry, little beast, and he threw a wild energy into this race against time. Down the slope and on with steady sweep, he sped as speeds the light. On—on, over rough road and narrow street, through swirling dust and turbid acequia. Once he pushed 200 yards up a callejon, or blind alley, and had to retrace his course; again, a Mexican policeman sprang into the road before him, waving his hand indignantly, but he smashed recklessly on, drowning the spiteful ineffectual crack of the officer's pistol in his rear. Swifter—swifter now, unfalteringly on he pounded, nor slackened the killing pace until his master drew him up with a jerk under the grim, gray walls of the battlemented Alamo!

Cordoña leaped to the ground, shoved his banderilla, or Mexican traveling shawl, up under his chin, pulled his cloak closely about him and accosted the sentry in well-simulated Spanish patois.

"Pardon me, señor; may I speak a word with Ross Kemble, please—one of the garrison?"

The other scowled and shook his head.

"Most important message, señor; friend of Señor Kemble dying," persisted the Mexican. Thinking better of it, the sentry stepped to the low, wide, sculptured door and transmitted the stranger's request.

"Señor Kemble, I believe?" said the latter interrogatively.

"Yes, who are you and what do you want?" He could not recognize the face or figure of the Mexican in the dark, nor recall his voice, having heard it but once before.

"My name is Felipe Rodriguez, señor, a poor vaquero below Mission Espada. While on my way to town this evening I was stopped by an old woman named Niña. She begged me to go into the house of her mistress, Señorita Burgess, a beautiful young lady, who was taken suddenly ill this evening. She was in bed, and asked me to be sure to come here and tell you that she wished to see you at once.

"Go, señor; I fear she will die! You may use my horse, which stands yonder, as I came in to see some friends and will not go back till close to midnight."

"Ill? Ruth Burgess ill?" repeated the American, astounded. "Why, man, I saw her only this morning and she did not complain of sickness."

"It was most sudden, señor. A faintness, a numbness, she says on the whole left side. It is paralysis, señor; no doubt, paralysis."

"Paralysis!" echoed Kemble, aghast.

Stunned by the ominous intelligence, he made no further inquiries. Hastily quitting his informant, he hurried to Colonel Travis, who, little dreaming of the on-creeping peril so near at hand, readily granted his request for two hours leave of absence. When he turned to the Mexican, he found him in the act of tightening the saddle girth. Standing aside to allow the American to mount, a faint gleam of light from the fortress quivered upon his face. Kemble fixed a quizzical frown upon him as he swung into the saddle.

"Man," he said, "I hope you are honest, and if so, you shall be well paid for your trouble; but if you have deceived me, beware! Adios!"

"Adios, señor! Do not spare the horse. Be quick!"

In a flash horse and rider were swallowed up by the forbidding shadows of the night.

"Fly, poor, unbelieving patriot! The truth would not serve you now. Doubt and frown if you must, but fly! fly! fly!" apostrophized Cordoña, peering south into the darkness. After the hoof falls had died out beyond the broad plaza, he heaved a deep sigh. Looking up at the cloudy sky, he touched the brim of his sombrero in token of military salute, and exclaimed:

"The strategy passes from my hands, O God! Quicken thou its results! Again I thank thee for that new light!"

With that he stepped briskly to the side of the sentry and, stooping, whispered something in his ear. Next moment erect of figure and alert of step, he was within the doomed fortress! In less than fifteen minutes from that time, a warning shot from the sentry announced the opening of the most thrilling drama in modern warfare. The Alamo was surrounded by the Mexican army under Santa Anna! . . .

Shortly after daybreak, on March 6, the Alamo was one vast, silent chamber of horrors. The ghastly dead were there in every conceivable attitude, and, among them, hard by the couch where the emaciated Bowie died, as if with characteristic devotion he had sought that spot to shield the invalid here, lay, his livid face upturned and hair—stiff, matted and gory—the sinewy form of Santos Cordoña!

When Santa Anna later stumbled upon the corpse he uttered a fierce exclamation of disgust, and, drawing a cavalry sword, ran it through the body. Then, sickened by the charnel odors of the place, he passed out of the east door of the fortress, wiped his boots on a clump of dewy grass, and threw a glance of fiendish triumph toward the early morning sun—dull, dismal, red—as though the burnished golden swords of yestereve were newly risen from a bath in blood.

— Richard Wallace Buckley, *San Antonio Express*, May 7, 1911

18.
Funeral Pyres along the Alameda

Where workmen are excavating for the cellar of a new building that will stand on the spot of one of the two funeral pyres whereon the bodies of those slain in the Alamo's defense were consumed is one of the memorable places of San Antonio, never marked and constantly passed unheeded. Few know that such a prominent event in history was there enacted. It will not be long before this spot and the one where the other funeral pyre was built will be the sites of buildings for commercial purposes, and the populace, in all probability, will forget that either place was ever of such historical interest.

The spot where the cellar is being dug comprises one-half of the area on which the first pyre mentioned was located. It is on the north side of East Commerce Street, adjoining the Ludlow House. The building is being constructed by Dr. G. H. Moody. The pyre occupied a space about ten feet in width by sixty in length, and extended from northwest to southeast from the property owned by Mrs. Ed Steves, on which the Ludlow House is built, to and through the property that the Moody structure is to occupy, and a short distance out into the street. The other pyre, which was on equal width, was about eighty feet long, and was laid out in the same direction, but was on the opposite side and on property now owned by Dr. Ferdinand Herff, Sr., about 250 yards southeast of the first pyre, this property being known as the site of the old Post House or the Springfield House.

The sites of the two pyres have been pointed out to me by several persons, three of whom saw them when the bodies were being burned and before the ashes had been scattered and the

fragments removed. These three persons are all living today. One of them is Enrique Esparza, who states he was a child eight years old when the siege and fall of the Alamo took place, and that he was in the Alamo with his parents and one of his brothers. He said that his father and the brother mentioned were killed in the Alamo and his mother and he were taken before Santa Anna after it had fallen. Esparza says that Mrs. Dickinson, the wife of Lieutenant Dickinson, . . . was taken with her infant to Santa Anna at the same time as also was Mrs. Alsbury and several other women and children.

Santa Anna gave each of the women two silver pesos, or Mexican "dobe" dollars when he ordered their release. Esparza says:

> After this we went to look for the body of my father and my brother, but when we got to the Alamo again all of the bodies had been removed and taken to the Alameda. They were put in two piles, one on each side of the Alameda, and burned. All of the dead killed in the siege who were defenders of the Alamo were burned, both Mexicans and Americans, and my father and brother were among them, but we could not find them in either pile, for the soldiers would not let us get close enough to examine or claim them.
>
> They set fire to them and burned them. My mother placed her mantilla before her face and ran screaming from the scene, dragging me by the hand with her. After the bodies were burned we went back several times to the two places until all of the fragments had been removed and the ashes had been scattered in every direction.

The next one to show me the two places was old Don Pablo Diaz, also still living, who said:

> My parents fled with me. I was a child then. I had a brother older than I who espoused the cause of Santa Anna and fought in his army. After the Alamo had fallen we returned to town from the Calaveras, where we had gone. On our approach we saw a huge pillar of flames and smoke shooting up to a considerable height to the south and east of the Alamo. The dense smoke from this fire went up into the clouds and I watched it while the fire burned for two days and two nights. Then it subsided and smoldered. During this time we had been hiding in the southern part of the city and left our retreat coming back to town by way of Garden Street.
>
> I noticed that the air was tainted with a terrible odor from many corpses and that thousands of vultures were circling in the sky above us. They were hovering over the city and especially along and above the river's course. As I reached the ford of the San Antonio River at the old

Lewis millsite I encountered a terrible sight. The stream was congested with corpses that had been thrown into it.

Ruiz, the alcade at that time, had vainly striven to bury the dead soldiers of Santa Anna's command who had been slain in the struggle during the siege. After exhausting every effort and all of his resources, he was unable to give burial to but a very limited number, these principally being officers. Being unable to bury them in the earth he was compelled to dispose of them otherwise. He had them cast into the swiftly flowing stream. But they were so numerous that they choked up the stream, finding lodging along the banks of the short curves and bends of that stream.

They obstructed the stream for some time until Ruiz was able to get a sufficient force to push the bodies away from the banks as they lodged against them and floated them down the stream for a considerable distance below, where they remained until devoured by the vultures and wolves.

I stopped and looked at the sickening sight, which made me shudder, and I became ill. I was told afterward that the sight and stench had even nauseated Santa Anna himself so that he had complained and reprimanded Ruiz for not getting rid of the dead. Involuntarily I put my hands before my eyes and turned away. But I could not even then help seeing the corpses. I turned away from the river which I hesitated to cross, and went to the right along the settlement of La Villita, but even then could not help seeing the corpses, for they lined the river's course and banks all the way from Crockett Street to more than a mile below.

But while the bodies of the Mexican soldiers in the river were a revolting spectacle the one that met my vision later was even more gruesome. It filled me with the greatest horror. I had passed along La Villita to South Alameda. This was a broad and spacious place used as a promenade and also as a highway of ingress to and egress from the city on the east side of the river. It has since become a part of East Commerce Street. On each side of the Alameda was a row of large cottonwood trees. From them the place took its name of Alameda. It commenced at about where St. Joseph's Church now stands, this having been the western extremity about half a block from South Alamo Street.

It was Santa Anna himself who had given orders to Ruiz to have the bodies of all who perished while defending the Alamo incinerated. By intuition I went straight to the place. I did not need a guide. The whole story was told by the spectacle I saw. The witnesses were silent but eloquent ones. They were the charred skulls, fragments of arms, hands, feet and other members of the bodies of the dead defenders. In carts the slain, among whom were Travis, Crockett, Bowie, Bonham and Jameson, as well as all of the others, had been removed from the Alamo mission, where they fell, to the Alameda, where they were burned on two different pyres. These were about 250 yards apart and one was on each side of the Alameda. The one on the north side was the smallest, while that on the south side was the largest. The latter was probably about twenty feet longer than the former. Both were about the same width—about eight or ten feet.

Both pyres were about ten feet high when the flames were first kindled, and the consuming of the corpses commenced. In the alternate layers the corpses and wood were placed. Grease of different kinds, principally tallow, was melted and poured over the two pyres. They were then ignited and burned until they burned out, leaving but a few fragments of different members. Most of the corpses were entirely consumed.

When I reached the spot I saw ashes, as well as the blackened chars of the different anatomical fragments. They emitted an odor even more sickening than did the corpses of those who had been thrown into the river and to me were much more nauseating.

Don Juan Antonio Chavez, also living here now, who saw the remnants of the pyres and the fragments of the bodies, was the third eyewitness who showed me the same spots that the other two did and confirmed their stories, all three coinciding.

Antonio Perez and August Biesenbach also showed me the same places and stated they had been the ones whereon the bodies had been burned. Biesenbach said that some of the fragments of heads, skulls, arms and hands had been removed and buried after being buried beneath the pyre at the Ludlow and Moody site.

They had been taken many years later to the Odd Fellows Rest, on Powder House Hill, and there given final burial, together with the bodies of several other persons who had been killed or died later, and had first been interred where the Alamo defenders' bodies had been buried.

I went with Biesenbach to the cemetery mentioned and he showed me the place where they were said to have been buried cbetween two tombs. These two tombs had monuments to people killed in tragic episodes which occurred some years after the struggle at the Alamo, and had no connection with it, but happened to have been buried for some time below the location of one of the pyres. When they were removed some of the fragments of those whose corpses were burned on this pyre may have been found, removed and buried, as stated by Mr. Biesenbach and other credible citizens, between the two tombs in the Odd Fellows Rest. . . .

There was an orchard very near the place where the bodies were burned on the south side of the Alameda, and it is stated that flames and sparks blowing in the fierce March wind that prevailed a part of the time during the incineration blew the flames into the orchard injuring many and destroying some of the fruit trees, most of which died soon after.

This fact probably gave rise to the prevalent belief that retained for many years, that after the bodies were burned none of the fruit trees in the neighborhood would bear and that they as well as the cottonwood trees all died soon after.

It is a fact that there are now no bearing fruit trees within a block of where either of the two pyres were, and there are but two of the fifty or more cottonwood trees left that grew originally on the Alameda. Neither of them is within a block of either of the pyres.

— Charles Merritt Barnes, *San Antonio Express*, March 26, 1911

19.

The Strange Devil – A Legend of Mission Concepción

Jack Radley, my old Harvard chum, was an ardent searcher after the bizarre and the romantic. He was not satisfied, however, to confine his search to fiction; he would willingly travel 1,000 miles to be on the scene of some strange, romantic drama and there gather its thrilling details from the lips of those who had participated therein; and, being young, rich and idle, he could indulge this whim to satiety.

I have been privileged to accompany him on several of his eccentric trips over the country and I felt no surprise when, on a mild evening in the spring of 1887, he asked me to go with him on what seemed to be a rather aimless trip to the South: "I want to take you to San Antonio, Texas, old boy—the Florence of America—and as irresistibly magnetic as the land of the lotus eaters. Can you break with the blandishments of New York for a fortnight to go?". . . .

"Pack up and be ready tomorrow evening. And----" with a catch of embarrassment, "bring your dress suit along. You will surely need it. San Antonio is a very social place, and I made some warm friends while I was down there, you remember, six years ago. . . ."

The day after our arrival in San Antonio I saw very little of Jack. He came to dinner, however, and with a flush of satisfaction on his dark handsome face, said: "Bob, I have arranged to present you to Col. Solon Baker tonight, the old gentleman of whom I spoke on the train. He promises to meet us at Concepción, near which he lives, to tell us of a weird happening there over fifty years ago. The hour he appointed is 11 o'clock; I have ordered a cab to be at the hotel for us at 10. . . ."

The appointed hour saw us seated on the trunk of a fallen tree with a venerable, white-bearded man between us. A few feet distant were the decaying walls of the old church of Concepción, well-nigh hidden from view in a vesture of woodbine, wild grape and climbing ivy, while some 200 yards farther on was a grove of pecan trees, at the western verge of which stood a large adobe cottage, the home of Colonel Baker and his family. The light of the moon falling through the leaves of the huge trees played tremblingly upon a gay group of children gathered about a young lady who was entertaining them with guitar and song.

Then in clear, convincing, though low and sepulchral, tones that harmonized well with the spectral shadows cast by the old ruin before us, the Sage of Concepción began the legend:

Walter Russell was the dearest friend I ever had. Both of us were vigorous, high-spirited young men, fresh from college, when we first met at a rural gathering among the mountains of Tennessee, way back in the early '30s. Russell was of a cheerful, amiable disposition, but inordinately fond of adventure, and, being like myself, bereft of kith and kin, we decided to follow Sam Houston to Texas. Side by side we fought for Texas liberty against the despotism of Mexico; and when the arch-tyrant Santa Anna went down in ignominious defeat on the banks of the San Jacinto, we still kept our arms and led a life of adventure on the plains, settling down eventually in this town. . . .

There lived at that time on Garden Street, in the vicinity of the old Mill Bridge, the daughter of one of the defenders of the Alamo. The loveliness of character and beauty of person of this young girl captivated the heart of Russell. After a short courtship he proposed marriage, and was accepted. The wedding took place at the bride's home one calm evening in early autumn. How can I ever forget that ill-omened marriage—or dismiss from my memory the awful incident that clouded what could have been the moment of supreme felicity for my friend?

The minister had just begun the nuptial service when there swept into the bridal parlor a young woman of extraordinary demeanor . . . her black eyes distended, her breast heaving like a tempestuous sea, her raven hair falling in disarray over her face and shoulders. With a species of demoniac imperiousness she threw up her hand and demanded a cessation of the ceremony so that she should be heard.

Then gazing with infinite scorn upon Russell who, pale as a ghost, had turned to face her, she shrieked: "Who are you to stand where you are? May the curse of heaven be upon you tonight! Yes, a black avenging curse upon you—you ravager of a woman's honor, vile, smoothfaced, hypocritical man. . . . My earthly prayer is that I may be the instrument after death. . . . Good-by, till we meet again!"

She waved her arms frantically, as if bidding those present farewell, backed toward the door, snatched a vial from her bosom, swallowed its contents and fell to the floor, writhing in an agony of death. We bore her to an adjoining chamber and laid her on a couch, where she expired almost immediately. Russell dispatched a servant to her relatives, whose address he knew, after which the wedding ceremony was resumed, but it seemed to have merged into some horrible dream.

Who was she, this strange, seemingly demented Mexican maiden that had blown in like a gust from the grimy, suffocating pits of Gehenna to smother the wonted merriment of a wedding hour? Madelina Mora!—Madelina Mora! Yes, that is the name, that is written on my memory with a stylus of fire.

From that night Walter Russell was a changed man. He grew listless, haggard, emaciated. Constitutionally brave, even to rashness, as I often saw him in the face of danger, he now became morbidly timid, and was at all times enveloped in a sickly mist of melancholy. Much concerned for his welfare, I urged him to give me the reason for his changed condition.

It was then that he confessed to me, with evident relief, the story of his former infatuation for beautiful Madelina Mora, the descendant of cultured Castillian ancestry, of the love he had unwittingly kindled in her bosom and his final resolve, for reasons of his own, not to marry her. Although I felt that he reserved something of his secret from me, he impressed me with the firm conviction that, in his intercourse with the unfortunate girl, he had not seriously swerved from the path of honor. Poor Walter! I am glad to think that of him now.

"Even so, Walter," I reasoned feelingly, "why allow this unhappy being to disturb your future? Why mope about forever in the shadow of this gloomy memory?"

"Solon," he replied, "I cannot help it. I feel like a ruined man. I haven't sufficient energy to take hold of the most trifling affairs of business. You know that I have never been superstitious, yet, I am overpowered at times by the feeling that some frightful catastrophe is to end my days—an inevitable catastrophe that no human agency may avert and that is being hurried toward me from the mysterious world of spirits." He tottered and began to tremble violently.

"My God!" he exclaimed suddenly, as he peered along the river bank near which we stood, "did you see anything there, under the cypress trees?" I looked, but saw only the swaying trees and a glint of the dying sunset on the gently flowing river. "Come away from this spot," he urged, endeavoring to suppress his agitation. "I boated with her along the stream at this point on the first evening of our acquaintance."

I took his arm as we strolled away, seeking to pacify him as best I could by earnest appeals to his reason and the virile manhood that I knew he possessed. I entreated him to shake off this unmanly illusion and made light of, even ridiculed, his grim forebodings. I was pleased to observe that my efforts were not entirely fruitless. He parted from me in a spirit of composure and self-confidence.

We resided in opposite parts of the town, and I did not see him again for a month. Then, one dull, sultry evening in June, he called upon me. Unfolding a sheet of paper, he handed it to me, requesting my perusal of its contents. As nearly as I can remember, it read as follows:

> Sir: This note will introduce its bearer, Don Antonio Gomez. I have just arrived in San Antonio, and for the first time am made acquainted with the villainy you practiced toward my sister. Explanations are superfluous. There is but one honorable course open to me. If you are a man of courage, which I much doubt, please name some friend to arrange with Señor Gomez the preliminary steps for a meeting. Permit me to state in conclusion that if you do not fight I will kill you on sight as I would the

vilest cur that breathes. Señor Gomez is quartered at the Hotel Alameda. Till we meet, Manuel Mora.

Before I had time to make any comment Walter handed me his reply, which read:

Sir: Your scurrilous note has, indeed, rendered an explanation on my part superfluous. I have designated Solon Baker as my second in this matter, and have directed him to call upon Señor Gomez without delay.

When I looked up from the paper he said: "Pardon me, Solon, for framing this answer without consulting you. You will serve, however, will you not?"

"With pleasure, Walter," I returned, almost choked with indignation when I thought of Mora's insulting language, "but who is this brother—the challenger?"

"A captain in the Mexican army. He was under General Urrea in the cowardly massacre at Goliad."

"Then may an avenging God give him to the demons! I will see his man at once," I said, rising to order my horse.

I had no difficulty in finding Gomez. Our conference was brief. A duel with swords was agreed upon for our principals, to take place the following night at 10 o'clock, in yonder grove upon which we are now gazing. The moon was to be at its full, and, the spot being remote, we had no fear of interruption.

Well, the morrow dawned clear and bright, but toward dusk a violent storm broke over the town. Its like I have seen but once or twice since. The rain continued to descend in huge white sheets, with no sign of intermission. I saw that some alteration in our plans for the duel would have to be made. About 9 o'clock, therefore, I again sought Gomez, who flatly informed me that the meeting must take place that night or be indefinitely postponed, as his principal had engaged, if alive, to leave the following morning by stage for Mexico.

In this predicament, my mind hit upon a plan. I was familiar with the secret, subterranean passage that ran from the Alamo to the Mission Concepción, a distance of some two miles. It was tunneled in earlier days by the Franciscan missionaries and their flocks, as an avenue of escape from marauding hordes of savages that every now and then swept over the town like a besom of destruction.

"Why not use this tunnel, effect an entrance into the church of Concepción and let the encounter take place there?" I proposed.

"Very well, very well," replied Gomez, "I will so notify my principal, and I can assure you that he will be satisfied."

"I can give the like assurance on the part of mine," I returned promptly. "Come to the Alamo with Mora at 10 o'clock. Bring two lanterns. Adios, Señor; be punctual!"

"Never fear," he answered, "adios!"

That night we made our way through the dark, dank, dungeon-like tunnel in silence, like a quartet of Quakers, while the hoarse thunder and the crashing rain blended their voices in ominous chorus overhead. At several places on our journey the ground was sodden from the water that penetrated deep fissures in the earth above us, and at others we were compelled to stoop and crawl where the upper and lower strata of humid soil touched each other, in large seams, resembling the cicatrix of a wound. Altogether our experience was one probably never paralleled before or since.

At length we emerged through an iron gate covered with brushwood, in the rear of the mission, and hurried within. Heedless of the sacrilege, we lighted the candelabra and prepared for the combat. Walter Russell had thrown off his coat, and, sword in hand, stood in one corner of the church. He beckoned me to him. Much to my surprise he seemed very cool—the Russell of old. Grasping my hand, however, he said gravely:

"Solon, I have a presentiment that this night will be my last. In this event, be the comforter and protector of my beloved wife and a father to my unborn child. Farewell, dear friend, my antagonist awaits me."

With that, he strode hastily, but firmly, to the middle of the aisle, where Mora stood on guard. "Set your mind on death, villain, for by heaven, I intend to send your guilty soul before its accusing victim—my ill-fated sister! Ready!" cried the Mexican in a tone of scorching malice. Russell instantly advanced to meet him. Both were excellent swordsmen, fencers of unusual talent, but as often happens in such cases, the battle was of short duration.

Mora was the larger man; Russell more wiry, supple and of steadier nerve. Clash followed clash; there were several alternating lunges and parries in rapid succession, when the Mexican missed, by a hair, a vicious plunge for his adversary's body. That was his undoing. The next instant, ere he had regained his poise, Russell's blade of cold steel slipped through his throat from ear to ear! The vanquished duelist reeled foward and fell.

Then there came a moment—one single, swift, terrible moment—that all the puny philosophy of naturalism can never blot from my mind! What was it—the shape—that specter, indescribable because it must have crossed the line of our vision at some point beyond the ordinary avenues of consciousness, which dashed in from the blustery night, heralded only by a lurid lightning flash, and sprang toward the victor?

Russell gave three terrific shrieks and staggered back—his mouth foaming, eyes starting from their sockets, his quivering swordhand sweeping the weapon before him like a scythe, in a futile effort to ward off the fearful object. But Gomez and I saw no more. We were struck as dumb as Saul on the road to Damascus. I was first to recover, and shaking like a leaf, roused my companion from his stupor.

One terrified glance sufficed to show us that Russell was as dead as Mora—his head lying in a pool of blood, his sword piercing his throat in a manner identical with that of his late antagonist!

Aghast, Gomez and I fled the church and the churchyard. Ignoring the darksome tunnel, we trudged home over the muddy Mission Road, the rain having abated considerably. Early next morning the good padre of the mission, horror-struck, discovered the impious, ghastly tragedy and reported the matter to the authorities.

I made no public statement of the case until years later. It is true, however, that I broke the news to Mrs. Russell as gently and tenderly as I possibly could. She was a delicate girl, though brave, and bore up well. Two months after her husband's tragic end she gave birth to a posthumous child—a boy. The mother died about twenty years ago, and the son, now dead also, married and became the father of a lovely girl. When bereaved of both parents, I took

the child, Lucille Russell, into my own family, loyal to the trust, thank God, imposed upon me by her lamented grandfather on that fateful night over fifty years ago.

With a sigh of mingled self-righteousness and sorrow, the aged speaker arose from the tree trunk, glanced at his watch, and walked softly over to the sculptured window of the decaying mission. He stood still for a few minutes as if listening, then came slowly back and said:

Friends, so strong was the image stamped on my mind that awful night that I occasionally go, even now, to the side of the church half fancying, although I realize how unreasonable it is after this lapse of years, that I may again hear the echo of the soul-freezing screams of my long lost friend. For months after the tragedy, at this hour, I heard that echo—muffled like the tones of a distant bell—but unmistakable.

Now, what was the supernatural visitation that caused those shrieks? I ask again, as I will ask till my voice is hushed in the silent halls of death. Could Madelina Mora's unquenchable thirst for vengeance, even beyond the portals of the tomb, have given her spirit sufficient power to effect some subtle materialization, enabling her to accomplish the dread purpose of her wrath by causing her distracted victim to pierce his own throat with his sword? Such things, they say, have happened.

The impressions of Gomez and I were as variable and incoherent as those of two revelers on cocaine might have been. I am satisfied, therefore, that our subsequent ideas of the hideous specter lie outside the orbit circumscribing the faculty of memory; they were merely illusions caught from the dim realm of dreams. The mystery belongs doubtless to that shadowy region of psychic phenomena where play the innumerable forces of which we can have no cognizance while our perceptions are limited to the five senses—the normal modes of consciousness.

The sage had finished his story. We sat silent, lost in the depths of the mysterious. Over the meadow, through the fragrant air, floated low, sweet notes of the guitar. Presently the look of mystic abstraction faded from Jack Radley's face. He rose smiling, waving his white handkerchief as though signalling the fairy group in the grove. The young lady I had been comparing to Diana among the nymphs came pirouetting in. Taking her hand, Jack said: "Forgive my want of conventionality, Bob, and allow me to present you to Miss Lucille Russell; Lucy—" turning his radiant face to hers, "this is Bob Merritt, my dearest friend."

Blushing, she bowed to me, then looked up at Jack and blushed more deeply still. Joy, hope, light, love, beamed from the countenance of my friend, while over the old man's wrinkled visage there passed a smile of mingled pride and love.

As for me, long inured to the eccentricity of my college chum, I did not marvel; neither was the presence of the dress suit in my trunk at the hotel any longer a mystery. Jack Radley, lover of the romantic, and Lucille Russell, child of a weird, tragic romance, were married the following night.

— Richard Wallace Buckley, *San Antonio Express*, April 30, 1911

21.
Skeletons Tell a Story

At every step in the progress of the demolition of the old Garza home and the work of replacing it with a mammoth modern structure by its present owner, Edwin Rand, in the excavations and tearing away of the walls, objects of interest are uncovered, many of them evidences of mysteries that in the unraveling unfold romance and history of exceeding attraction.

Last week, besides the finding of a sword and a bayonet, supposed to have played a part in the combat incident to the capture of San Antonio by Milam and his men, and a cannon ball, probably fired during the same hostilities, were found a pocket knife of ancient make, an old stirrup such as was worn by the grandees of Spain at the time of the coming of Cortez and an old broadax similar to the axes of the executioners who beheaded Cordero, Sauceda, Herrera and other prominent Spanish officials here in early days. Two skeletons were likewise turned up by the plowshare. . . .

But the story revealing the identity of the two persons whose frames in life they formed is even a thrilling one, and there is no doubt whatever as to the truth of the story, for it comes . . . straight down through the Garza family and has been revealed to this writer by Don Leonardo Garza, Sr., the head of the old de la Garza family, who has preserved the relics and history of the family back for more than seven centuries and of the events and persons connected with that illustrious family, mention of whom has frequently been made in former articles.

One of the skeletons found was that of a female, while the other was that of a male. The one of the female showed that the person whose frame it was had been one much younger than that of

the male had been. Likewise it showed that the body formed about the skeleton of the female had been buried at a somewhat later period than the corpse of the person containing the male skeleton was.

In tracing back the history of events noted in the chronology of the Garza family, Mr. Garza ascertained that in the year 1812 there was a widow, whose name was Donna Juana Barcenas, who lived on the east side of Soledad Street next to the Veramendi Palace. She had two children, a boy and a girl. Both of this widow's offerings met with tragic ends, the girl being the first to perish. She died that year, while the boy was drowned in a great flood of the San Antonio River in 1819.

The skeleton of the female was evidently that of the girl. Her name was Maria en Gracia Barcenas, or Mary in Grace Barcenas. She was about 16 years old and very beautiful. She had many suitors for her hand, and many of the prominent young men of the time paid her court. She was a great favorite of the Garza family. Although Maria's mother was quite poor and Maria earned some of the means of supporting her mother by serving the Garza family about the house, she was not considered in the light of a servant, for she was of noble lineage and she, as well as her mother, were considered friends and equals of the family.

One night while Maria was sitting in the patio of the Garza palace listening to the sounds of the lute or mandolin of one of her suitors, the wild and piercing sounds of an Indian war whoop were heard not far away. She jumped to her feet and ran to close the portals of the immense porte cochere on Acequia Street.

She had swung one of the pair of doors shut and was in the act of closing the other when the party of Indians reached the front of the gate. One of the savages, seeing her, placed an arrow in his bow, drew it back to the head, and aiming at the girl, let it fly. It found lodgment in her bosom. The arrow pierced her heart and she was caught in the arms of her suitor as she was falling, and died almost before the echoes of the sounds of the notes of the guitar had faded and the love song was still fresh in her ear. . . .

While those about the fair corpse wept, a posse was formed and went after the Indians. The Indians lurked about the town for some days watching to catch any straggling person whom they might find wandering about the suburbs, so it was determined unsafe by the mourners to bury the body of Maria in the cemetery, which was at that time on the outskirts of town, although the place where it then was is where the Santa Rosa Hospital and Milam Square are now, near the city's present center. As there was already a grave in the garden of the Garza palace it was determined wise to bury her corpse beside that which already reposed there. So the grave was consecrated by the priest, who then performed the funeral rites. . . .

The story of him who in life tenanted the frame found beside that of the young girl is also one of great interest. During the last years of the eighteenth century there came from England a gentleman of elegance and refinement, who for a short period stopped in New York, but afterward went to New Orleans. There he remained until he, with several others, left the Crescent City and came to San Antonio. This gentleman's name was John Walker. Those with whom he came were the Compte de la Baum and two other French gentlemen, Monsieur Gillette and Monsieur Vidal. They reached here in the year 1786. . . .

He and his companions formed acquaintance with the then head of the Garza family, Don José Antonio de la Garza. Walker became not only a friend but a guest of Don Antonio, who invited him to become one of his household and assigned him quarters in his "tapanco" or garret. In those days all Anglo-Saxons who happened to come to this locality were called "pirates," although they may never have been buccaneers in any sense of the word. That was the term that Santa Anna applied to the Americans, and all not of the Latin race who located in Texas during his regime and in all probability was the term given all Americans, English and German people by the Spaniards and the Mexicans in those early days.

At any rate, although called a pirate, there is no authentic history of Walker which in any way connects him with piracy, or any act bordering on it. He was warmly and highly esteemed, lived a very exemplary life and died within a very short time after coming here. He, however, was not of the Roman Catholic faith and the only cemetery then here was that of the Catholics, who refused burial of any therein not of that faith, so when John Walker died at

Don José Antonio de la Garza's house, the latter did not want to see him buried inappropriately and therefore had the corpse placed in a grave in his garden not far from what was then Rivas Street, but now Houston Street. . . .

By the Mexican people Walker was known as "Juan Guacca," instead of John Walker, Juan being the equivalent in Spanish for John in English and "Guacca" . . . phonetically as closely resembling the word Walker in Spanish as they could pronounce it. Walker had but little to say concerning himself and kept very closely to himself and his garret, except when walking about the town or sitting at the table or in the patio of the palace of his host and friend, Don José Antonio de la Garza.

But when he came to San Antonio he brought an antique chest which contained his few belongings, but into which no one except himself ever looked until long after he had died and had almost been forgotten. During the exciting times incident to the Civil War this old chest, which was securely locked, had been taken from the "tapanco," or garret, of the Garza palace to the Garza ranch at the confluence of the San Antonio and Medina Rivers. It remained there undisturbed until after the war when it was brought back from the ranch and replaced in the "tapanco," when in 1868 it was opened by Leonardo Garza, who found in it the effects of its former owner, John Walker. He knew very little about John Walker except that his father had mentioned him and his coming to San Antonio at the time mentioned and having been given a home with the family and buried on the premises.

Mr. Garza sought Ramasio de los Reyes, who owned a ranch not far from the Garza ranch, who had known Walker well, and who told Leonardo Garza what he knew of Walker's history, and which has been related here. . . .

The statement that there is a store of treasure buried beneath the old Garza palace excites deep interest in the excavation now going on there, especially since the bodies that Leonardo Garza said were buried there have been found and other interesting objects have also been unearthed there. The theory that there is treasure buried there is made very plausible by the fact that some years ago, when a partition wall was being torn down a very considerable quantity of treasure was there found, consisting of coins amounting to many thousands of dollars.

There is an expectation that a secret passage connecting the Garza with the Veramendi palace will be found, but this is not likely to be realized for the reason that when the Veramendi was demolished no such passage was discovered, and for the further reason that there is no reasonable ground for believing that any such secret passage existed.

The theory that there were secret passages connecting these two places and the Alamo as well as some of the old missions down the river has been considered for some time, but it is more likely that this theory is based on the revelations of old abandoned and long disused irrigation ditches that were walled up when built and which were filled up after abandonment.

These ditches have been found on Alamo Street, on Garden Street, on Main Plaza, Houston Street and along other thoroughfares. They had been out of use so long that their former existence had been forgotten. The fact that they ran directly in line of the places mentioned led to belief that they went to the Alamo, the Veramendi and the missions below the city, but even if the theory of the secret passages is fallacious, there have been enough true discoveries made to give glamor to the historic old places demolished.

— Charles Merritt Barnes, *San Antonio Express*, June 16, 1912

22.

The Curious Story of a Woman and a Turkey

It is a strange tale, the principal characters in it being a woman and a turkey. About a year ago there was a wedding at the Mission Espada. The contracting parties were two Mexicans, the man named Antonio Ximenes and the woman Elisa Valdez. . . .

It is in one of the adobe buildings at Espada that Elisa Valdez is living, almost under the shade of the mission's weather blackened walls. A lithe and pretty dusky faced girl, with luminous eyes and a mass of coal-hued hair, that falls over her shapely shoulders to her uncorseted waist. She lives with her grandmother, Benita Salazar, an old lady whose face has the marks of Father Time's etching needles, and whose mind is richly stored with the traditional lore of her race.

When Antonio Ximenes first courted Elisa Valdez she was a widow. Her first husband had wooed and married her within a week, and then a month later he left for Mexico to go to his grave. How he came to his death it matters not.

Soon after she was a widow, Antonio pressed his suit, which was at first treated with indifference, for Elisa loved her dead husband and was true to his memory. Antonio's passion for the young widow was but increased by constant rebuffs, and he was persistent. He was good looking, generous, and had a small farm a few miles from the mission; his constant ardor at last brought its reward, and Elisa consented to marry him.

Happily and with swelling heart Antonio went to the parish priest Father Bouchou, telling the kind old man the good news and instructing him to publish the banns. Father Bouchou congratulated the young man, whom he knew to be hard working and honest and sincerely in love with the granddaughter of Benita Salazar. For three consecutive Sundays were the names of the engaged couple read out to the small congregation that assembled weekly in the mission church and at length the morning which was to see the consummation of Antonio's hopes arrived.

That same trinity of bells that with vibrant tongues would send forth their messages of prayer across the wild prairie in days long past rang out with merry clangor from the time worn campanile for the nuptials of Antonio and Elisa. The little church was crowded with those who lived in the settlement. There was the grandmother, her wrinkled face peering out of a shawl that covered her head; beside her, the uncle, who was reputed well to do in the Espada community; and then the bride looking more complacent and unconcerned than the groom, whose face beamed with a smile of realized anticipation.

The ceremony was soon over and as man and wife they repaired to the adobe dwelling of Mrs. Benita Salazar, escorted by their friends. The day was passed in feasting and merriment.

As night fell and the moon arose, a musician from San Antonio came out and joined in the general jollity and soon the strains of his guitar were to be heard in fantastic waltz melodies to which everybody danced. Antonio and Elisa had not been a moment by themselves, for the old grandmother persisted in keeping the girl at her side and, with the contrary garrulity of age, kept talking about the virtues of Elisa's dead husband until the newly made wife became sad with past memories of her first love.

Whenever Antonio approached she waved him away with her stick, telling him she wanted to have Elisa as long as possible to herself, she was the only kith on earth she cared for. In deference to the dame's request Antonio would leave the pair to join the dancers.

Still in Elisa's ears came the monotonous sound of the grandmother's voice, always the same burden, until at last the girl left her with a feeling of miserableness and heavy presentiment. She wanted to be alone and unobserved. She stole out through the back of the house, leaving the gay crowd who were celebrating her marriage behind. In solitude and moonlight she breathed easier, but the strange restless feeling at her heart made her wander on and on. Finally to her ear came the voice of the musician, who was singing in that nasal tenor characteristic of his race. Clearly the words came to her:

Toma el arpa con que canto,
Las asanas de los Reyes
Y de amor las dulces leyes
De tu imperio seductor.

The girl shivered as if with cold, although the air was laden with heat. She felt something pull her dress from behind. Thinking someone had followed her, she turned round with an impatient gesture, only to see a large turkey plucking at her. Her heart stood still, for Mexicans of the lower order still cling to the doctrine of metempsychosis. Like the Indians they believe souls of their departed relatives enter into bodies of birds and beasts after they have quitted their own frail clay tenements.

The turkey plucked at her dress again and uttered its guttural gobble. She moved away affrighted, but the turkey followed her crying louder, and catching hold of her dress dragged her in the direction of the house. Almost fainting with superstitious fear, she halted as conviction forced itself on her. It was her dead husband come to upbraid her for her forgetfulness and faithlessness to his memory. She placed her hands before her eyes, remorseful and penitent.

In a second her mind was made up, and a determined expression was on her face as she removed her hands and glanced around to see where the turkey was, for it had ceased pulling her gown. It was not to be seen; she was by herself; only the hum of insect music and the distant jingle of a guitar was to be heard.

Elisa walked back rapidly to the dwelling. As she neared it her husband approached her. "I have been watching for thee, sweet Elisa; we have missed thee," said Antonio. As he spoke he placed his arm around her waist and bent foward to kiss her. As Elisa felt his warm breath on her face, the sound of a turkey's voice caught her ear and with a frenzied movement and distended eyes she dashed away from Antonio and ran like a deer to her grandmother's arms while Antonio, bewildered and puzzled, walked back slowly, pondering on Elisa's strange freak.

An hour later Antonio was dashing madly over the prairie on horseback, the reins were held by listless hands and he let the animal go where it would. The mesquite thorns would scratch his face, but he never felt them. His horse stopped at length with so sudden a jerk that it almost threw him from the saddle. It was then he tried to arouse himself from the stupor that had come over him. He passed his hands over his brow trying to collect himself only to find he had lost his hat, that his face was bleeding from numerous scratches and that he was before his own door.

He could not tell how it all had happened. He only knew that Grandmother Salazar had told him Elisa would not go home with him, she did not want to be his wife. He had laughed at first and went to find Elisa. She was crouching in a corner. As soon as she saw him she uttered a cry and ran out into the night. He had followed and overtaken his wayward bride when she turned on him with eyes blazing like those of a tigress and struck him full in the face with her hand. Then she turned away and dashed toward the house ere he could recover his breath.

"It is not good," Grandmother Salazar had said when he returned, "Elisa is your wife but she will not go home with you, don't worry the child now, as she is too excited."

It was then that Antonio had mounted his horse and with face still smarting from Elisa's blow, rode off, he cared not whither.

All this occurred a year ago, and Antonio Ximenes has no wife in his house although he is married. Elisa is still living with her grandmother. Antonio is as deeply in love as ever but when he sees her she flees at his approach. Prayers and entreaties are of no avail. Elisa will not go to him. The only one she seems to heed is old lady Salazar. She tries to intercede for Antonio, uselessly, however, the girl is firm. She wanders around the mission and the vicinity tending to her goats and her only pet, a large turkey over which she sings sweet Mexican love songs.

A few days ago, Antonio Ximenes went to Justice Chavagneux, justice of the peace for that district, from whom these facts were ascertained, and asked him to see if he could prevail on Elisa to come to his home. Justice Chavagneux consented and went to Mrs.

J CISNEROS

Salazar's house but he met with no better success. Elisa would not listen to him. She walked off followed by her pet turkey toward the Mission Espada. Her uncle and other Mexicans say the girl has eaten of the Ialvache weed, but when Elisa hears this, she shakes her head and croons over her feathered companion.

— *San Antonio Express*, July 4, 1888

Index

Index   135

Donald E. Everett is professor of history emeritus at Trinity University, where he chaired the history department from 1967 to 1981 and received several awards for teaching and research. His work in newspaper archives uncovered a trove of lore—including that in *San Antonio Legacy*—now considered basic to understanding the region's colorful past. He graduated from the University of Florida in 1941, completed his M.A. and Ph.D. degrees at Tulane University and is the author of several books on San Antonio and Texas history.

The drawings of José Cisneros, a longtime resident of El Paso, have been published in more than fifty books, among them his *Riders Across the Centuries*, *Faces of the Borderlands* and Francis Fugate's *The Spanish Heritage of the Southwest*. In 1969 the University of Texas awarded him a residence fellowship at J. Frank Dobie's Paisano Ranch, where he completed *Riders of the Border: A Selection of Thirty Drawings*. In 1993 he was the subject of John O. West's *José Cisneros: An Artist's Journey*.